P9-AQM-879

TO CLOTHE THE NAKED
and Two Other Plays

LUIGI PIRANDELLO (1867-1936) was born in Girgenti, Sicily. He attended the University of Rome and took a doctorate in philology at Bonn University in 1891. Pirandello began his literary career as a poet, but he soon turned to fiction and in 1904 published his first widely recognized novel, *The Late Mattia Pascal.* With the appearance of *It* Is *So!* in 1917 Pirandello proved himself to be one of the most original and powerful dramatists of the 20th century, a claim well substantiated by his two greatest plays, *Six Characters in Search of an Author* (1921) and *Henry IV* (1922). Pirandello opened his own Art Theatre in Rome in 1925, and was awarded the Nobel Prize in 1934.

TO CLOTHE THE NAKED

and Two Other Plays

BY

LUIGI PIRANDELLO

To Clothe the Naked
The Rules of the Game
The Pleasure of Honesty

Newly translated into English
by
WILLIAM MURRAY

NEW YORK
E. P. DUTTON & CO., INC.
1962

FIRST EDITION

Published simultaneously in Canada by Clarke, Irwin & Co., Ltd., of Toronto.

First published in Italy under the following titles:
VESTIRE GLI IGNUDI *(To Clothe the Naked)*, 1923
IL GIUOCO DELLE PARTI *(The Rules of the Game)*, 1919
IL PIACERE DELL'ONESTÀ *(The Pleasure of Honesty)*, 1918

Library of Congress Catalog Card Number: 62-10055

To E. W. Swackhamer,

who did a great playwright

full justice

CONTENTS

Introduction ix

To Clothe the Naked 3

The Rules of the Game 79

The Pleasure of Honesty 143

INTRODUCTION

Ultimately, no one can speak for a writer but the writer himself, and Pirandello was painfully aware of this simple truth. Writing to a friend, Domenico Vittorini, in 1935, he commented that "the world of international literary criticism has been crowded for a long time with numerous Pirandellos—lame, deformed, all head and no heart, erratic, gruff, insane, and obscure—in whom, no matter how hard I try, I cannot recognize myself, not even in the slightest degree." I do not wish to add another freak to this gallery, so I offer this brief introduction not as the final word on Pirandello's plays, but only as a modest attempt to achieve some kind of perspective on the man and his work, especially in relation to his present status in this country. After all, Pirandello's philosophy, his ideas, his observations on life and the difficulties of living are all there, readily available and clearly stated in his work. It is dangerous for the critic or the translator to presume to paraphrase or simplify them. "If so many believe me erratic," the playwright wrote, "it is because I move in my own way and not as others would like me to."

Of the great philosopher-playwrights of the past hundred years, Pirandello is perhaps the least appreciated in the United States. Two or three of his forty-four plays, especially *Six Characters in Search of an Author,* are performed every year by small dramatic groups, but first-class professional productions are few and far between. Nothing of his has been seen recently on Broadway and very little in the smaller theatres of off-Broadway. During the season of 1960-61, for instance, in New York, supposedly the theatre capital of America, there were only two productions of any consequence: Stage Society's presentation of *The Rules of the Game,* in my translation, and the Living Theatre's *Tonight We Improvise.* The former had a six-weeks run, and the latter survived for several months as part of a weekly repertory. The year before, there were no productions of any consequence at all in New York. No Pirandello play, on or off Broadway, has ever, to the best of my knowledge, enriched an American producer. Yes, everyone agrees, Pirandello is unquestionably a very great playwright, but the American public will not buy tickets to his plays. Why not?

The answer is not so obvious as it might seem. It simply isn't true that the public will not support the modern classics at the box office. Chekhov, Shaw, even Ibsen have enjoyed successful revivals recently. There clearly should be enough of a public for Pirandello as well. The expense-account audience of Broadway, of course, is absolutely beyond redemption, but it would be wrong to assume, as I believe many people do assume, that Pirandello speaks such an odd, convoluted, and abstract language so outside the mainstream of current American thought and experience that he has nothing relevant to say to us. On the contrary, I believe that with his concern for human truths, for the essential, eternal ideas and values that lie at the root of Western man's social and private behavior, Pirandello's work has never been more pertinent than it is today. If there is as yet no substantial audience for him here, then one will have to be created, despite the fact that, with one or two exceptions, there is almost no really perceptive dramatic criticism in our popular press.

Pirandello's plays do not concern themselves with social reform, political evolution, or religious inquiry. In this respect, and in this respect alone, he is closer to Chekhov than to Shaw or Ibsen. Pirandello never placed any hope in man's ability to work out his salvation through group action or private faith. He never took a stand against fascism, for example, because he was indifferent to it; he would have created his theatre, or tried to at least, under any sort of political regime. Primarily, he was concerned with man, with the individual as a human animal torn between his instincts and his reasoning powers. "We ride through life on the beast within us," Angelo Baldovino says in *The Pleasure of Honesty*. Pirandello sees us as desperately and precariously balanced between our blind desires and our social obligations, unable to distinguish between the real and the unreal, treading a thin, dangerous line between insanity and conscious suffering, seeking and never finding a solution to the mystery of life itself. This is why his plays, unlike quite a few of Shaw's and Ibsen's, are still vital and important. They have nothing to prove, they offer no solutions; they are merely dedicated to stripping us of our lies, our deceptions and illusions, in order to arrive at some naked truth about ourselves. It is important to note, too, that there is no character development in any of Pirandello's plays; he is exclusively, to an extent matched only by Shaw, the playwright of ideas.

In all of Pirandello's plays there is inevitably a character who speaks directly for the author, who explains and comments on the action, even though he may be directly involved in it. This character almost always operates on two levels: on the one hand he is an integral part of the drama, on the other he will tell you what the drama is really about. Thus, in *The Pleasure of Honesty*, Angelo's behavior is what brings about the dramatic denouement, but to bring it about he is forced to explain to the other characters in the play (and, therefore, to the audience) why he and they are acting as they are. He tells them not only what they feel, but why they feel it, and what they would feel if they fully understood the truth of the situation. In *The Rules of the Game,* Leone tries to remain completely out of the action from the start, but it is as a direct result of his apartness that the crisis of the play occurs. He explains, he warns, he tells everyone what they must do and not do, he proclaims himself indifferent because uninvolved. Of course, he is not uninvolved; Pirandello shows us that by the mere act of living, the fact of existence, a man cannot help but affect the lives of others. In *To Clothe the Naked,* Ludovico Nota begins the play by bringing Ersilia home to live with him, but, as soon as life becomes too complicated and intrudes noisily into the peace and quiet of his rooms, he also attempts to remove himself, proclaims himself a disinterested bystander, and spends the rest of the play off to one side, commenting illuminatingly on the drama.

In the hands of a mediocre writer this technique could prove disastrous, since nothing can be duller than having someone in a play constantly explaining and editorializing at the expense of the action, and it has to be conceded that not even Shaw could be more wearisomely didactic than Pirandello when he occasionally wanted to make too certain that the audience understood every nuance of the dramatic text. Fortunately, Pirandello was not a mediocre writer, and because of the complexity of his ideas and the brilliance of the language in which he expressed them, one rarely becomes overly conscious of the basic artificiality of this method. (To any such criticism, indeed, the playwright could quite justly reply that the stage itself is an artifice.) Pirandello's spokesman is usually by far the most interesting character in the play, and it is to him that one listens with the closest attention. If his language sometimes seems too abstract, it is because the playwright's world is a world of ideas, and ideas are the abstractions by which we claim to live.

In my opinion, however, it is the use of this familiar, easily recognizable dramatic technique that has done more than anything else to keep Pirandello from establishing lasting contact with his potential American audience. The more complex a playwright's ideas are, the more abstract his language, and the lengthier his speeches, the more difficult he is to translate, and Pirandello, alas, wrote in Italian. No other playwright has suffered as much in translation as he has, and even in his own lifetime he was well aware of it. He once went so far as to equate translators with traitors: "*Traduttore, traditore,*" he quipped to a friend. And in reading over some of the early English translations of his plays, it is impossible not to sympathize with his bitter remark.

It is not so much that his translators distorted and betrayed his work (though one of them took the liberty of adding several lengthy speeches) as that they simply failed to capture in English the quality of Pirandello's writing. At its best his language is precise and clear, stripped of ornamentation even at its most torrential, and at times, by its very simplicity, it achieves a beauty that raises it to the level of poetry. (Consider, for instance, several of Leone's long speeches in Act 1 of *The Rules of the Game*, speeches that almost sing, so meticulous is the playwright in his choice of words.) Ideally, a translator must not only be faithful to the playwright's intention, but he should also, in his own language, re-create the original. That is not always possible, often because the translator just isn't up to it, sometimes because, especially in works of a strong regional flavor, there is no equivalent music in another tongue. In this latter connection, one thinks of D. H. Lawrence's heroic but doomed attempt to cope with

Verga's Sicilian tales, but, if one excepts *Liolà* and two or three of the one-act plays, Pirandello poses no such problem. His texts are fortunately free of the speech mannerisms of regional dialects, so that it becomes reasonably safe to blame the translators for the shortcomings of the English versions of his plays.

I am not here presenting my own efforts as perfect examples of what can be done with Pirandello, but I do say that in translating these three plays, I benefited to some extent from previous examples of how *not* to translate them. For instance, here's a short speech from an earlier translation of *The Pleasure of Honesty*:

> BALDOVINO: I am like a person trying to circulate gold money in a country that has never seen anything but paper. People are inclined to suspect that gold, are they not? It is quite natural. Well, you are certainly tempted to refuse it here. But it's gold, Signor Marchese, I assure you —pure gold—the only gold, by the way, I have never been able to spend, because I have it inside me—in my soul and not in my pockets. If I had it in my pockets—

Although this translation is fairly accurate as far as meaning is concerned, it is a labored job, stilted and awkward. Read aloud, it does not have the sound of a human voice speaking a living language. After all, Pirandello wrote dialogue intended to be spoken on a stage to an audience, and it is part of the translator's task to make that dialogue sound authentic, as if the speaker had thought of it and spoken it at the very moment of conception. This is one of the secrets of successful drama. Who would pay any attention to Shakespeare's plots and characters if the plays were written in pedestrian verse? Who would listen to Shaw's discourses on politics and society if the words did not crackle and flash in the air around us? If Ibsen and Chekhov and Pirandello were great playwrights, it was surely not only because they were philosophers and men of compassionate wisdom, but also, and to an equal extent, because they were artists and poets. Whatever the defects of my own translations, I offer them in the hope that I have at least benefited by the mistakes and omissions of my predecessors.

Of the three plays in this collection, one, *To Clothe the Naked,* is an authentic masterpiece. Under the title *Naked,* it has already been translated several times and has been produced twice in New York, but never in a first-class theatre. On both occasions neither the press nor the public responded enthusiastically to the play and it enjoyed only brief runs. It is not hard to understand why. The play is extremely difficult to do well, requiring not only a good translation but also absolutely topnotch acting and direction. It unfolds very slowly, bit by bit, meticulously, scrupulously, as if the playwright were dissecting a living organism, cell by cell, in order to arrive at last at the very heart of the matter, Ersilia's pathetic secret, which, Pirandello tells us, is also everybody's secret. Anything less than a first-class production inevitably defeats this work, because it is so carefully constructed and balanced, because it does require as much from its cast and director as it gives. It can pose some fearful traps for the actor, as I realized only too well when I attended a reading of the play a few months ago. Some very expert and talented Broadway actors attacked the text as if it had been written by William Inge, pausing where no pauses were indicated, adding words, subtracting others, embellishing their interpretations with gratuitous dramatic touches. The result was that the first scene between Nota and Ersilia took forty minutes alone and the play as a whole became as long-winded as *Parsifal.*

No Pirandello play can withstand this sort of treatment,

but *To Clothe the Naked* is particularly vulnerable simply because it has been so carefully written. From its interpreters it requires intelligence, imagination, absolute respect for the playwright's intention, the mood he wishes to evoke (and Pirandello's stage directions are most explicit here), and the words he has written. Above all, it requires a style of ensemble playing that seems to have vanished, if it ever did exist, from the American theatre. It is probably true, as some critics have pointed out, that the first act could stand a bit of judicious pruning, but it would be extremely risky to attempt it until the play is well into rehearsal and the cast has fully familiarized itself with it. On the whole, *To Clothe the Naked* is not the play I would recommend for production by a small theatre group, even though its technical demands are modest—seven actors and a single set. Under the right circumstances, however, I am convinced that the play would make a tremendous impact and be recognized here, as it has been abroad, as the great work of art it unquestionably is.

The other two plays, *The Rules of the Game* and *The Pleasure of Honesty,* are closely linked, both in subject matter and style. In fact, the central character in each play is really the same man, one of those brooding, tortured, supremely logical intellectuals Pirandello so often provides to explain and motivate the action. Leone in *The Rules of the Game* has abstracted himself from life and from the pain of being alive, by imagining it as a game in which the players must choose a part and play it to the hilt, right to the very end, and which can only be won by the person who understands the rules and acts only from certain predetermined concepts. "In other words, my friend," he says, "the secret of living is to find a pivot, the pivot of a concept on which you can make your stand." In *The Pleasure of Honesty,* Angelo Baldovino escapes from life by actually embodying a concept supposedly held by others, the concept of honesty. "I exist only in what seems to be," he tells his best friend. "Sometimes I'm amazed at the sound of my own voice, the echo of my own footsteps through these rooms; to discover that I need a drink of water or feel the need to rest. I live—do you see?—deliciously, in the absolute of a pure abstract form."

Neither play is on quite the same level as *To Clothe the Naked,* but each has virtues of its own. The dialogue is brilliant and often extremely witty, even though the playwright's intention remains essentially a serious one; the characters are fascinating and sharply etched, each one a slightly grotesque projection of Pirandello's angled, penetrating view. We are shown the absurdity of life, we are made to laugh at ourselves, but quite suddenly the playwright will turn on us and reveal that the laughter is hollow, that the absurdity is tragic, that life may indeed be a game but that death is always the last move in it. At the end of *The Rules of the Game* Leone stands silent and motionless, impaled on his pivot by the reality of Guido's fate. In *The Pleasure of Honesty* Angelo yields to Agata and to life, but he feels no joy in the surrender; he knows that his marriage and his fatherhood will bring him a measure of suffering as well as pleasure. This play is one of the few in all Pirandello's work that ends happily, which may account for its immense popularity in Europe, but it is not the happiness of a soap opera, not even the gay despair affected by Jack Tanner in *Man and Superman.* Unless the audience understands that Angelo would really have preferred to escape from his commitments, the ending degenerates into pure sentimentality.

I think it would be impossible to deny that Pirandello was essentially a pessimist, but in this he is hardly unique. Which of our great writers would we acclaim as an optimist? Nor should his pessimism be confused with the nihilism of a writer like Jean Genet, for instance. He was above all else an artist, a man who wrote in order to show us the real face we choose to hide daily behind the masks we assume to disguise ourselves from ourselves and from others. And though Pirandello was always conscious of universal suffering and the inescapable reality of the grave, he was not blind to the light nor untouched by joy. At the end of his letter to Vittorini he wrote: "A man, I have tried to tell something to other men, without any ambition, except perhaps that of avenging myself for having been born. And yet life, in spite of all it has made me suffer, is so beautiful! And here is another positive statement without even a shadow of logic, and yet so true and deeply felt . . ."

WILLIAM MURRAY

TO CLOTHE THE NAKED

and Two Other Plays

TO CLOTHE THE NAKED
(Vestire gli ignudi)

CHARACTERS

ERSILIA DREI
LUDOVICO NOTA
MRS. ONORIA
ALFREDO CANTAVALLE
FRANCO LASPIGA
EMMA
GROTTI

ACT I

The combination study and living room of the writer, Ludovico Nota, in Rome. Afternoon.

ACT II

The same, the following morning.

ACT III

The same, late that afternoon.

TIME: *The present.*

ACT I

The combination study and living room of the writer, Ludovico Nota. It is a large, shabby room cluttered with books, magazines, papers, and odd pieces of furniture, all at variance with each other. On the walls hang second-rate paintings and drawings by the author's artist friends, and there are many overflowing bookshelves. The over-all impression is one of disorder and the kind of fading gentility one associates with reputable rooming houses. An exit leads into the bedroom, another into the rest of the house and, eventually, the front door. Despite two large windows, the room is usually dark because it is on one of the lower floors, the street outside is narrow, and the houses opposite cut off the light. Whenever these windows are left open, the turbulent noises of the crowded street invade the apartment, but even when they are closed one is always conscious of the harsh, brutal life outside.

At Rise

The room is empty, the windows are open, and the noises of the street are clearly heard. Ersilia Drei now enters and stands inside the door as if unaware of her surroundings. She is quite decently dressed, like a governess or a school-teacher, but her clothes are slightly worn, a little faded. She is not much more than twenty years old and beautiful, but, having just barely escaped a brush with death, she is very pale and her eyes are lost in shadow. Still on her feet and obviously waiting for someone else, she looks about the room. She makes an attempt to smile, a little sadly, at what she sees, but the street noises disconcert her.

Ludovico Nota finally enters in the act of putting his wallet back in his pocket. He is a handsome man in his fifties, with bright, piercing eyes and a ready youthful smile. Although he does his best to be affable, he is by temperament a cold, thoughtful man, entirely devoid of the natural warmth that easily invites the sympathy and confidence of others. His attempts to be jocular and friendly are so artificial that they often embarrass and disconcert people.

LUDOVICO: Here I am! Sit down, sit down. Oh, these windows are a curse! *(He rushes to close them.)* But if I don't leave them open, it gets so stuffy in here. You know how it is with these old houses. Please, please, take off your hat. *(Ersilia does so.)*

(Mrs. Onoria enters from the bedroom holding a pile of dirty laundry under one arm and a broom in the other. She is about forty: a short, dumpy woman with dyed hair and a suspicious, ill-tempered face.)

ONORIA: Excuse me.

LUDOVICO *(surprised)*: Oh, you were in there?

ONORIA *(spitefully)*: I put clean sheets on the bed. That's what you asked me to do in your note this morning.

LUDOVICO *(embarrassed)*: Ah, yes.

ONORIA: But if it's for— *(She looks at Ersilia and breaks off.)* Mr. Nota, I think it's time we reached an understanding. I'll just take these things downstairs and—

LUDOVICO *(drily)*: That's decent of you.

ONORIA *(angrily)*: Who are you to talk about decency?

LUDOVICO: Well, I only meant that you ought to get rid of that dirty laundry before—

ONORIA: I'm going to get rid of all the dirt around here!

LUDOVICO: What do you mean by that?

ONORIA: I mean that girl, for instance. And you talk to me about decency, bringing one of her kind into my house—

LUDOVICO: By God, you keep a civil tongue in your head or I'll—

ONORIA: You'll what? We're going to have this out once and for all! I'll be right back! *(She exits hurriedly.)*

LUDOVICO *(moving after her)*: Dirty-minded old gossip!

ERSILIA *(dismayed, holding him back)*: No, no, please! I'll go.

LUDOVICO: Not at all! This is my house!

ONORIA *(reappearing)*: Your house? What do you mean, your house? Rented rooms, that's what they are! And get it into your head that this is a respectable place, run by a lady!

LUDOVICO: You? A lady?

ONORIA: Yes, me, me! Who else?

LUDOVICO: You're certainly proving it!

ONORIA: Yes, I am! Because I won't allow you to fill my house with your women!

LUDOVICO: You insolent slut!

ONORIA: You watch your mouth!

LUDOVICO: A slut, a slut with a filthy mind who doesn't know who she's talking to, that's what you are!

ERSILIA: Please . . . I've been sick . . . in the hospital . . .

LUDOVICO: Don't waste your time explaining anything to her!

ONORIA: Sick, are you! Well—

(The noise of a heavy truck passing in the street drowns out her words and rattles the windows.)

LUDOVICO: That's enough of this. She's going to stay here for a few days and there's nothing you can do about it.

ONORIA: There isn't, eh? The rooms were rented to you, not to anybody else!

LUDOVICO: What if my sister came to visit me? Or some other relative?

ONORIA: They can go to a hotel!

LUDOVICO: Do you mean to tell me I'm not free to put her up here for a few nights?

ONORIA: This girl is no relative of yours!

LUDOVICO: How do you know she isn't? And suppose *I* went to a hotel?

ONORIA: Well, you should have asked my permission first. And politely.

LUDOVICO: Ask your permission? Imagine that!

ONORIA: Yes, and politely, too! And since you're always complaining about the rooms and how stuffy they are, why don't you move out? Why don't you?

LUDOVICO: I intend to. And soon. Now get out.

ONORIA: You'll really leave?

LUDOVICO: Yes, in a few days. At the end of the month.

ONORIA: Fine. I won't say another word.

LUDOVICO: Good. Now get out.

ONORIA: I'm going. I'm going. Don't worry. Not another word. *(She exits.)*

LUDOVICO: Can you imagine! I'm so sorry. No sooner do you set foot in here than we have this lovely scene.

ERSILIA: Oh, that's all right. It's really my fault, sir. I shouldn't have—

LUDOVICO: No, I've been fighting over a year with that old witch. Tied here, I don't know, by the weight of all this rubbish. Perhaps you thought . . . well, the home of a writer . . .

ERSILIA: No, I don't mind. But it's too bad that you, I mean, famous as you are . . .

LUDOVICO: We'll move into a new place at the end of the month. I've already signed the lease. It's a lovely spot, near the park. We can go up and see it tomorrow, if you like. And then we can go and pick out the furniture together. I want you to build yourself a little nest with your own hands . . .

ERSILIA: No, really, I–

LUDOVICO: I would have had to get out of here anyway. You know, I'm one of those people who always have to make a fresh start. I'm so glad I had the inspiration to write to you and to begin this new life, now, with you. (*Indicating his surroundings.*) You know how it is: you feel yourself sinking into a swamp, you stagnate, you can't breathe. Then, suddenly, you look up and fill your lungs with fresh air. What was it? Nothing. A breath of wind and everything changes. That's what my life is like.

ERSILIA: I really don't know how to thank you, sir.

LUDOVICO: Well, you can begin by not calling me "sir." And anyway, it's I who ought to thank you for having accepted the little I could offer.

ERSILIA: Oh, no! It means so much, so much to me. If you only knew, sir!

LUDOVICO *(smilingly correcting her)*: Ah, what did I say?

ERSILIA: I'm sorry. I'll have to get used to it. I–I'm so grateful.

LUDOVICO: Grateful? Why?

ERSILIA: Because I was so lucky that someone like you . . .

LUDOVICO *(teasingly)*: You mean a famous writer?

ERSILIA: I mean that my story, appearing in a newspaper, my last desperate act, should have won for me the consideration, the pity–

LUDOVICO: The interest, the interest!

ERSILIA: –of a man like you.

LUDOVICO: Yes, when I read about you in the paper I was, well, fascinated. You know, you stumble by chance into something, or someone drops a casual remark and suddenly, I don't know, you feel something–a wave of sympathy, a moment of understanding–and before you know it you have the germ—the germ of a story, of a novel—

ERSILIA: That you want to write about me?

LUDOVICO: No. Try to understand. I don't want you to think it was just professional curiosity on my part. I only mentioned it so you'd realize how I happened to become interested in you.

ERSILIA: But if my life, all those terrible things, all that unhappiness, at least served to—to—

LUDOVICO: To help me write a novel?

ERSILIA: Why not? I'd be so happy, so proud. *(Smiling, she goes up to him.)* Really.

LUDOVICO: *(after a pause)*: You leave me quite speechless.

ERSILIA: Why?

LUDOVICO: Because, without wanting to, you make me feel very old.

ERSILIA *(confused)*: I do? But I didn't mean . . . I only—

LUDOVICO: My dear, I don't want to write a novel; I want to live one! I told you I was fascinated, but not because I wanted to write a book. I hold out my arms to you and, instead of your lips, you offer me a pencil and a piece of paper.

ERSILIA: It's—it's too soon—

LUDOVICO: For your lips—I know. Or is it too late?

ERSILIA: No.

LUDOVICO *(noticing her embarrassment)*: Isn't it strange how differently we each react to the situation? I was offended that you could think my interest in you was motivated only by a writer's professional curiosity, while you, instead, are offended—or at least unhappy, admit it—to hear that a writer, a real writer, if he wants to write a novel, doesn't have to make the offer I made or come and fetch you home from the hospital to do it. The moment I started to read about you in that newspaper, the novel began to take shape in my head, all of it, from beginning to end.

ERSILIA: But how? So quickly?

LUDOVICO: In a single instant. And in such a wealth of events, in such detail . . . Oh, it was marvelous: the oriental setting . . . that little villa by the sea . . . you there as governess . . . that little girl falling from the terrace . . . their sending you away . . . the trip back . . . your arrival here . . . the sad discovery . . . all of it, all of it . . . just like that, without ever having seen you or spoken to you.

ERSILIA: You imagined me, but how? How? Like this? The way I am? *(Ludovico smilingly indicates no.)* How then? Tell me. Please.

LUDOVICO: Why do you want to know?

ERSILIA: Because I want to be as you imagined me.

LUDOVICO: No, I like you much, much more the way you are! I mean, for myself, not for the purposes of that novel.

ERSILIA: But then . . . what should have been a novel about me became a novel about someone else?

LUDOVICO: Of course. The girl I imagined.

ERSILIA: Was she very different from me?

LUDOVICO: Somebody else entirely.

ERSILIA: Oh, but then . . . I don't understand, I don't understand any more—

LUDOVICO: What?

ERSILIA: Your interest. How can you be interested in me?

LUDOVICO: Why not?

ERSILIA: If I'm not the girl you imagined, if the things that happened to me, all the things you read about in the paper—I mean, if you imagined them happening to someone else, someone who has nothing to do with me — *(She pauses, bewildered, troubled.)*

LUDOVICO: Well?

ERSILIA: Then–I'd better go.

LUDOVICO (*laughingly*): Not at all, my dear. The girl in my novel, we'll send her away! Not you!

ERSILIA (*suspiciously*): Not me? I don't belong in the story? You didn't believe me, then?

LUDOVICO: Of course I believe you! But now I want to imagine you in a new life, the life you can have with me. And I want you to imagine it, too–a new life, free from the memory of all the terrible things that have happened to you.

ERSILIA (*with the ghost of a smile*): Then . . . not the girl in the novel . . . not the way I am . . . but still another?

LUDOVICO: Yes, another, the one you can become.

ERSILIA (*turning to him, amazed*): I? (*Bowing her head, with a very slight helpless gesture of her hands.*) I've never been anything.

LUDOVICO: Oh, now, you don't mean that.

ERSILIA: Nothing . . . ever . . .

LUDOVICO: But you're–you're–

ERSILIA: What?

LUDOVICO: Well, first of all, a beautiful girl.

ERSILIA (*sadly, shrugging her shoulders*): Beautiful? No. And then I've never known how to use my looks.

LUDOVICO: Ah, when you don't know that . . . Yes, I can see it all now . . . You could even do something desperate . . . one last attempt before the end . . . you give up, you let yourself go . . .

ERSILIA (*looking at him, fearfully*): Oh, God! What are you saying?

LUDOVICO: Nothing. I was imagining it, imagining what the girl in the novel might do. Desperate, at the end of her resources . . . toward evening . . . she looks at herself in the mirror of that dismal little hotel room . . . a sudden decision, a mad temptation . . . She has nothing left, hardly any money . . . the hotel bill to pay . . .

ERSILIA *(amazed, terrified)*: But none of this was in the paper, was it?

LUDOVICO: No, I was just– *(He looks at her, surprised.)* Why? It's true?

ERSILIA *(hiding her face in her hands and trembling with shame)*: Yes.

LUDOVICO *(almost to himself, pleased)*: Well, well, how accurately I envisioned it! *(Then once more sympathetic, anxious.)* You went down into the street that night?

ERSILIA: Yes . . . yes . . .

LUDOVICO: And . . . and it was with someone you picked up? Just anyone who came along?

ERSILIA: And . . . and afterward . . . I didn't know what to do . . .

LUDOVICO: How to ask him for money? *(When Ersilia doesn't answer, he continues.)* And so he gave you nothing, eh? Nothing. Ah, how rightly I guessed it, all of it! And then the loathing, the horror at the failure of this last sordid attempt . . . Perfect! Perfect! *(Ersilia begins to sob.)* No, no, you mustn't cry. It's all over now. *(He starts to embrace her, to comfort her.)*

ERSILIA *(getting up, ashamed)*: Let me go. Please let me go now.

LUDOVICO: Go? Why?

ERSILIA: Now that you know . . .

LUDOVICO: But I knew already!

ERSILIA: How?

LUDOVICO: I imagined it! Don't you see? I imagined it all. And I was right.

ERSILIA: I'm so ashamed.

(At this moment there is a sudden burst of noise from

the street: the shriek of brakes, the sound of a collision, then screams, shouts, cursing, whistles, a honking of horns.)

LUDOVICO: No, you mustn't– *(He turns toward the windows.)* What the devil's happening?

ERSILIA: They're shouting . . . perhaps an accident . . . *(The noise increases, screams for help are heard. Onoria, frightened, enters hurriedly.)*

ONORIA: They hit an old man, a poor old man! Crushed him against the wall! Right under your window! *(She runs to open a window. Ludovico and Ersilia run to the other. When they open them, the noise becomes an uproar that fills the room. There has been a collision and one of the vehicles has pinned an old man against the wall of the house. The old man, either dead or dying, is surrounded by a shouting crowd, some of whom are trying to free him and get him to a hospital. The scene emerges for us through the shouts of the onlookers, among which we hear:)*

VOICES IN THE STREET: Oh, oh, God! God! Help him! Help him! The poor man! Crushed like that! Get back there! Who did it? Who did it? Where's the driver? He's gone! No, there he is! Get him! Get him! He's dead! An old man! Hurry up! Hurry up! Watch out! Don't let him fall! Against the wall! He's dead! I tried to turn! I couldn't help it! It's his fault! He blocked the road, I would have hit him! Liar! You were going too fast! Arrest them both! Murderers! All right, all right, let's give him a little room there! No, he's dead! Dead! The poor man! Hurry up! Hurry up! Get him to the hospital! Up the street! Two blocks! His hat, don't forget his hat! The poor old man! Murderers! Murderers! *(The three watchers at the windows reflect in their movements the scene below them.)*

ONORIA: He's dead . . . dead! Oh, the poor man! Hey,

watch out there! Don't drop him! The driver tried to get away! Look at his face! Somebody hit him! Oh! Squashed him like a toad!

ERSILIA *(horrified, backing away from the window)*: God, what a sight! What a sight!

LUDOVICO *(closing the window)*: Some poor old man in the neighborhood, probably. Mrs. Onoria, close the window, please!

ONORIA: They're taking him away! He must be dead!

LUDOVICO: If not, he'll die on the way to the hospital.

ONORIA: I'm going down to find out how it happened! How dreadful! How dreadful!

(She exits hurriedly.)

LUDOVICO: In that narrow little alley, so dirty that when it rains you can't even walk in it, they drive their cars and trucks. And once a week the pushcarts come in and they turn it into a market place. Imagine!

ERSILIA *(after a pause, staring rigidly into space, afraid)*: The street . . .

LUDOVICO: And what an education for a writer! Instinctively your imagination tries to free itself of petty obstacles, it wants to soar among the clouds. But the street is always there, with its people passing by, the noises of its life—the life that others lead, apart from yours but always there, disconcerting you, interrupting you, entangling you, opposing and corrupting you . . . You and I, for instance, we want to be together, to compose our lovely fairy tale together. Well, suppose it had been me down there just now, under that car. What would be left for you up here? But you know what I mean: the unforeseen event, the unexpected blow. When that child fell from the terrace . . .

(A pause.)

ERSILIA *(absorbed, gently)*: To serve . . . to obey . . . to have nothing, to be no one . . . A servant's dress, faded and worn, that you hang each night from a nail in the wall. God, what a frightening thing to feel that no one remembers you, that no one thinks of you . . . In the street . . . I saw my whole life, I don't know, as if it no longer existed, as if I had dreamed it . . . everything around me, the few people who passed by, the trees . . . the park benches . . . and I no longer, I no longer wanted to be anything . . .

LUDOVICO: Ah no, you see that at least wasn't true.

ERSILIA: Why wasn't it true? I wanted to kill myself!

LUDOVICO: Yes! But in doing so you created an entire novel—

ERSILIA *(fearfully)*: What do you mean, created? Do you think I made it all up?

LUDOVICO: No, no. I meant, in me. You created it in me, without knowing it, by telling your story.

ERSILIA: When they found me in that park—

LUDOVICO: Yes, and then later, in the hospital. Forgive me, but how can you imply you were nobody? For one thing, you existed in the pity everyone felt for you when they read your story in the paper. You can't imagine the impression it made when it was published, the interest you aroused all over the city.

ERSILIA *(anxiously)*: Do you still have it?

LUDOVICO: What?

ERSILIA: That newspaper. I want to read it. Do you still have it?

LUDOVICO: Yes, I think so. I must have saved it.

ERSILIA: Find it, find it! Let me see it!

LUDOVICO: No, why should you get all upset again?

ERSILIA: Let me see it! Please! I want to read it, I want to read what they wrote about me.

LUDOVICO: What you told them, I suppose.

ERSILIA: I don't remember exactly what I said. I hardly

knew what I was doing. Let me see it. Please find it.

LUDOVICO: Who knows where I put it? In this mess . . . Let it go for now. Later we'll look for it together.

ERSILIA: Did it tell everything?

LUDOVICO: Oh, you had three full columns at least. You know how it is in the summer: things are slow, then some reporter hits on a case like yours, it's sensational enough, and they fill up a whole edition with it.

ERSILIA: And what about him? What did they say about him?

LUDOVICO: That he jilted you.

ERSILIA: No, I meant . . . I meant the other man.

LUDOVICO: The consul?

ERSILIA *(startled)*: They said he was a consul?

LUDOVICO: Yes, our consul at Smyrna.

ERSILIA: Oh, my God, even the name of the city? They promised not to use it!

LUDOVICO: Well, you know newspapermen . . .

ERSILIA: But why did they have to do that? They didn't have to tell where it happened or who was involved. What else did they say?

LUDOVICO: That after the little girl fell off the terrace—

ERSILIA *(hiding her face in her hands)*: My baby! My poor little baby!

LUDOVICO: —he was ferociously cruel to you.

ERSILIA: Not him! His wife! His wife!

LUDOVICO: Both of them, it said.

ERSILIA: No! Only the wife . . . Oh, my God!

LUDOVICO: Because she was jealous of you. I can imagine. A great hulk of a woman—

ERSILIA: No! She was small—pale, thin, all shriveled up—like a lemon!

LUDOVICO: How strange! You know how I see her? Tall, dark, heavy eyebrows—I could paint her picture.

ERSILIA: Oh, you always see everything just the opposite! Who knows what you thought I was like? No, she's just as I said she was.

LUDOVICO: I'm sure of it, but, you see, for my purposes I needed a big woman because I pictured the child as being very thin, very delicate.

ERSILIA: She wasn't that way at all! My little Mimi!

LUDOVICO: I called her Tina!

ERSILIA: Tina? Mimi! Mimi was her name! A flower of a child! She used to run around the house on those fat little legs, her red cheeks, all those golden curls bouncing with every step! She loved me, only me!

LUDOVICO: And naturally that, too, must have made the mother jealous!

ERSILIA: Oh, yes. That more than anything else. And it was she, you know, it was she who, when the other man came, on the cruise—

LUDOVICO: The naval lieutenant?

ERSILIA: Yes. It was she who arranged everything that night, the night it all started. Leaving me there alone—on purpose—in that garden, drunk on the perfume of that night . . . the palm trees . . . all those flowers . . .

LUDOVICO: Marvelous! The sea, that hot sun, the warm tropical nights! What a setting! What a wonderful story!

ERSILIA: If it hadn't actually happened to me—

LUDOVICO: And that scheming witch! I can see it all! The treachery of someone who's never known happiness and who knows that the happiness she pretends to make possible for someone else will end in betrayal. Oh, it's perfect!

ERSILIA: If you could have seen her—like a mother to me—after he asked me to marry him. All the nice things she did for me . . . And then, after he'd gone . . . God, how can anyone change so quickly? Nothing I did was right, after me every minute . . . . And then she blamed me for the accident–

LUDOVICO: Whereas she was the one who had sent you out of the house on some trivial errand!

ERSILIA *(startled, turning to look at him)*: Who said so?

LUDOVICO: It was in the paper.

ERSILIA: That, too?

LUDOVICO: You must have mentioned it.

ERSILIA: No . . . I . . . I don't remember . . . I don't think I did . . .

LUDOVICO: Did I imagine it, then? Or perhaps the reporter dreamed it up in order to add a little color to the story, to point up the way they brutally turned you out of the house afterward, without even offering to pay your trip back. That part is true, isn't it?

ERSILIA: Oh, yes! Oh, yes!

LUDOVICO: Almost as if they expected to make you pay for the death of the child!

ERSILIA: And she threatened me, you know! Yes. I'm afraid she would have had me arrested if she hadn't been afraid that certain things would come out–

LUDOVICO: About her? Ah, you see, it's true!

ERSILIA *(anxiously)*: No . . . I don't mean . . . I don't want . . . In fact, I'm sorry if they wrote that it was she who sent me away. I–I don't want to think any more about what happened there . . . I'm thinking, instead, of the trip back, how I suffered. I had the feeling that the child was with me, on the boat, that she didn't want to stay with her cruel parents. . . . You know, I have the strangest impression: that I lost her forever that night, when I left the hotel.

LUDOVICO: But when you arrived here, didn't you try to find the man again?

ERSILIA: How? I didn't know his address. I wrote to him

in care of General Delivery. I even went to the Navy Department. They said he had left the service.

LUDOVICO: But you should have tracked him down. You should have made him pay for his betrayal, for what he did to you.

ERSILIA: I've never known how to stand up for my rights.

LUDOVICO: He promised to marry you!

ERSILIA: I didn't care any more. When I found out he was about to marry someone else, this last betrayal was too much, so unexpected that I—I just didn't care. I had no money left and . . . to go to him like a beggar . . . *(A pause, then staring into space.)* In the park, holding the poison in my hand, I thought only of the child. It gave me courage to think that, having lost her the night I went out into the street, I would soon find her again.

LUDOVICO: Now, now, now. Let's not think about all this any more. Come on, cheer up!

ERSILIA *(after a pause, with a sad smile)*: All right, but at least—at least let me be that other one!

LUDOVICO: That other one? Who?

ERSILIA: The girl you imagined. If just once I could be something! Just the way you said it was, in your novel, but with myself in it, exactly as I am! I'm sorry, but it's wrong for you to see anybody else in it!

LUDOVICO *(laughing)*: That's a good one! You feel I'm cheating you out of your story?

ERSILIA: Yes. Out of all the events, out of my very life itself. I no longer wanted to live; I suffered it all until I couldn't stand any more. And now I think I have a right at least to live in the story you'll make out of it—which will be beautiful, so beautiful, like that other novel I read of yours . . . wait . . . what was it called? . . . Ah, *The Outcast*. Yes, *The Outcast*. That's it!

LUDOVICO: *The Outcast?* No, my dear, you're mistaken. I didn't write *The Outcast*.

ERSILIA *(surprised)*: You didn't?

LUDOVICO: No.

ERSILIA: How funny! I thought . . .

LUDOVICO: As a matter of fact, it was written by Pirandello, a writer I particularly dislike.

ERSILIA *(mortified, covering her face)*: Oh, God!

LUDOVICO: Now, now. Don't be upset. You made a mistake, that's all. *(Ersilia begins to cry.)* You're not crying? Oh, come! What does it matter if you thought I was the author of somebody else's trashy novel?

ERSILIA: No . . . it's just that–that everything in my life is like this . . . Nothing–nothing ever works out for me. *(A knock at the door.)*

LUDOVICO: Who is it? Come in.

(Mrs. Onoria, now all sweetness and light, enters.)

ONORIA: May I? *(Looking for Ersilia.)* Where is she? *(She notices Ersilia drying her eyes and clasps her hands.)* Oh, she's not crying?

LUDOVICO *(amazed, not understanding the sudden change in attitude)*: What's the matter with you?

ONORIA: You could have told me she was the one in the paper! Miss Drei, Ersilia Drei, isn't it? The poor thing! *(To Ersilia:)* I'm so glad you're all right and that you're here with us now.

LUDOVICO: How did you find out?

ONORIA: Do you think you're the only one who reads the papers?

LUDOVICO: No, I mean that it was she?

ONORIA: Because the man from the newspaper, the one who wrote the story, he's here.

LUDOVICO: Here?

ERSILIA *(quickly, nervously)*: The reporter?

LUDOVICO: What does he want?

ONORIA: He wants to speak to her. He says it's important.

ERSILIA *(increasingly upset)*: Important?

LUDOVICO: Who told him she was here?

ONORIA: I don't know.

ERSILIA *(to Ludovico)*: I don't either! When I spoke to him, I had no idea I'd be coming here—with you . . .

LUDOVICO *(under his breath)*: Probably some busybody at the hospital— *(To Ersilia:)* What do you want me to do? Shall I let him in?

ERSILIA: No . . . I don't know . . . What could he want?

LUDOVICO: I'll find out. *(He exists.)*

ONORIA: You poor thing! If you only knew how I cried when I read about you!

ERSILIA *(ignoring her, very worried, glancing nervously toward the door)*: Now what can they want?

ONORIA: Maybe . . . who knows? . . . Maybe they—

ERSILIA *(in despair)*: I couldn't stand anything else!

ONORIA: Don't you feel well?

ERSILIA: No . . . I—I can't breathe . . . I'm not strong enough yet . . . It hurts . . . here . . . here . . . Oh, my God! *(A street organ suddenly begins to play, loudly and slightly off key, directly under the windows.)*

ONORIA: Here, loosen your dress.

ERSILIA: No, no. *(Disturbed by the music.)* Make them stop! Please!

ONORIA: Of course, of course. *(She fishes in her pocket for some change, runs to the window, and calls out to the organ grinder as she throws the coins into the street.)* Hey! Someone's sick up here! Go away! *(The music stops. Onoria closes the window and returns to Ersilia.)* All done! Now let's loosen your dress a bit.

ERSILIA: No . . . I have to be ready . . . I'm so afraid . . .

ONORIA: Of what?

ERSILIA: I couldn't stand it . . . If you only knew . . . The belt . . . so tight . . . *(She loosens the belt. The voice of Ludovico inviting someone to enter is heard outside the door.)*

LUDOVICO: No, no. Please, come in.

(Alfredo Cantavalle enters, followed by Ludovico. He is a pleasant, outgoing young man who does his best to appear far more sophisticated and blasé than he is. He has a round youthful face and tends to fat. His clothes are expensive, even elegant, but they don't quite fit him.)

ALFREDO: May I come in? Ah, my dear Miss Drei! Remember me? Alfredo Cantavalle, from the newspaper.

ERSILIA: Yes, I remember you.

ALFREDO: I'm so glad to see you again. *(Indicating Onoria.)* And the lady? A relative?

LUDOVICO: No. Just the landlady.

ALFREDO: Ah, of course. I remember. Miss Drei has no relatives. You had a bad accident out here, I understand.

LUDOVICO: Yes, an old man.

ONORIA: Right under our windows! It was awful!

ALFREDO: He's dead, you know.

ONORIA: He is?

ALFREDO: Yes. Died on the way to the hospital.

ONORIA: Who was he?

ALFREDO: They don't know yet. *(Turning to Ersilia:)* Miss Drei, we're to be congratulated, both of us! That I should have written your story and so brought your case to the attention of an illustrious man of letters—well, you can't imagine how happy I am for you!

ERSILIA: Yes, it really did bring me luck.

LUDOVICO: Please. It was nothing.

ALFREDO: It's been lucky for both of us, because now Mr. Nota can be our witness. And we may need his testimony. You see . . . May I speak freely? *(He indicates Mrs. Onoria.)*

ONORIA: I'll go, but be careful. She— *(Indicating Ersilia.)*

LUDOVICO *(to Ersilia)*: Don't you feel well?

ONORIA: She's sick.

LUDOVICO: What's wrong?

ERSILIA: I don't know . . . I don't know. . . . A chill . . . my nerves . . .

ONORIA: Now you listen to me! I'll take you in there and—

ERSILIA: No, no.

ONORIA: I'll put you to bed. You'll feel so much better in the morning—

ERSILIA: No, please. Leave me alone. I'm all right. I'm all right now.

ALFREDO: The effects of the poison, I suppose. But you'll see . . . with a little care . . .

LUDOVICO: And rest.

ONORIA: If you need anything, my dear, just call me.

ERSILIA: Yes, thank you.

ONORIA: I'll be downstairs.

ALFREDO *(nodding to Onoria)*: Madam . . .

ONORIA *(softly, to Ludovico)*: Be careful! Don't let her talk too much! Can't you see how she looks, the poor creature? *(She exits. Ludovico closes the door behind her.)*

ALFREDO: I'm sorry if my coming here—

LUDOVICO *(annoyed)*: It's all right, but please don't take too long.

ALFREDO: Two minutes, that's all I need.

LUDOVICO: Now, let's get to the point. What the devil does that fool of a consul want?

ERSILIA *(astounded, terrified)*: The consul?

LUDOVICO: Yes. *(To Alfredo:)* We'll have to settle with him once and for all!

ERSILIA: You mean he's here?

ALFREDO: Yes. He showed up at the paper yesterday and raised the roof.

ERSILIA *(to herself, despairingly)*: Oh, God! Oh, God!

LUDOVICO: And what does he want you to do?

ALFREDO: Why, only retract the whole story, that's all.

ERSILIA *(to Alfredo)*: You see? You see what you've done?

ALFREDO: I?

ERSILIA: I told you not to say where it happened, I told you not to use the right names! You promised you wouldn't!

LUDOVICO: A complete retraction? But how is that possible?

ALFREDO: Excuse me, sir, but I'll answer the young lady first, if I may. *(To Ersilia:)* Miss Drei, I didn't use his name. I mean, not his name, exactly.

LUDOVICO: You were absolutely right to unmask the man—

ALFREDO: All I said in the piece was "our consul at Smyrna." Who knows who our consul at Smyrna is? Certainly none of our readers. I didn't know who he was myself. The last thing in the world I ever expected was to have him fall on us out of the blue yesterday.

ERSILIA: My God! My God!

LUDOVICO: You mean he came back to Rome because of this?

ALFREDO: No. He came back because of the accident to the baby, because his wife apparently had some sort of breakdown. After what happened there, it was impossible for them to stay. It's understandable, of course.

ERSILIA: Yes, he told me so.

ALFREDO: He was here to ask for a transfer to some other post, you see. Then he read the paper and— *(He kisses the tips of his fingers.)* Oh, it's a mess, my dear sir.

LUDOVICO: Why?

ALFREDO: What do you mean, why? As a member of the diplomatic corps, his position is very delicate. In fact, he says his whole career is at stake. He's threatening to sue us for libel.

LUDOVICO: Libel? What did the story say about him specifically?

ALFREDO: It's all a pack of lies, he claims.

LUDOVICO: Lies?

ERSILIA: I still don't know what you wrote about him, or his wife, or the accident.

ALFREDO: I swear to you I only wrote exactly what you told me, no more, no less. Of course, in the heat of the emotion I felt for you I—well—but I didn't change a single fact or date. You can see for yourself, by reading the story.

LUDOVICO *(shuffling through the papers on his desk)*: I must have it here somewhere.

ALFREDO: Don't bother, I'll send you a copy. *(To Ersilia:)* Miss Drei, I'm sure you realize I'm only acting in our best interests. I came here to find out how we can defend ourselves against this man's threats.

ERSILIA *(leaping to her feet in an outburst of rage and indignation, speaking her lines through clenched teeth)*: He has no right to threaten, no right to sue anybody!

ALFREDO: So much the better, then, so much the better.

ERSILIA *(suddenly collapsing)*: Oh, it's so awful . . . so awful . . . *(She begins to cry again, obviously on the verge of hysteria.)*

LUDOVICO *(running to her, Alfredo following him)*: Ersilia! Ersilia! You mustn't!

ALFREDO: Miss Drei, please! Please! There's no need—

LUDOVICO: Ersilia, what is it? Please! Don't cry like this!

ALFREDO: There's no need to worry! Really!

LUDOVICO: She's fainting! Call the landlady!

ALFREDO *(running to the door)*: Mrs. Onoria! Mrs. Onoria!

LUDOVICO *(shouting)*: Mrs. Onoria!

ALFREDO *(exiting)*: Come quickly! The girl is—

LUDOVICO: Ersilia! Please! Get hold of yourself! It's nothing! Really! It's nothing!

(Alfredo returns, followed by Mrs. Onoria holding a bottle of smelling salts.)

ONORIA: Here I am, here I am! The poor child! There! Hold

her head up! Like that! The poor child! *(Holding the bottle to Ersilia's nose.)* I told you not to make her talk! I told you to leave her alone!

ALFREDO: There! She's coming around!

LUDOVICO: I think we'd better get her to bed.

ONORIA: Wait! Wait!

LUDOVICO: Ersilia!

ONORIA: There, there, you poor thing! It's all over now.

LUDOVICO: It's all right, Ersilia.

ALFREDO: It was nothing, Miss Drei. Really.

ERSILIA *(in a tiny, childish voice, almost gaily)*: Oh, dear! Did I fall?

LUDOVICO: No, why? You only threw a scare into us.

ERSILIA: I didn't fall?

LUDOVICO: No.

ONORIA: There, now, try to get up.

LUDOVICO: Like that. Slowly now.

ERSILIA: I thought I fell . . . as if, suddenly, I don't know . . . I felt so heavy . . . as if made of lead. *(Her eyes light on Alfredo and again she reacts violently, leaping to her feet.)* Oh, God! No! No! *(She staggers, again about to fall, but Ludovico and Onoria support her.)*

LUDOVICO: Ersilia, what is it?

ERSILIA *(turning away from Alfredo, trying to escape)*: Go away! Go away!

ONORIA: Yes, he's going! It's all right! We're here now! We're all here! *(She leads Ersilia toward the bedroom.)*

LUDOVICO: Yes, let's get her to bed. Let me help you.

ONORIA: Easy now, easy! We're all here! We'll have a nice long rest . . .

LUDOVICO: A good sleep and you'll feel so much better.

ERSILIA: I can't stand any more . . . I just can't stand any more . . .

ONORIA *(at the door, to Ludovico)*: You stay here. I'll take care of her. *(She exits into the bedroom with Ersilia.)*

LUDOVICO: You'd think they'd at least leave the poor girl alone now!

ALFREDO: I couldn't agree more. I feel so sorry for her. But you haven't heard the worst. There's something else she doesn't know about yet.

LUDOVICO: Something else?

ALFREDO: Yes. I'd better tell you. I heard it from the consul yesterday.

LUDOVICO: The consul? Tell that consul for me to go to hell!

ALFREDO: But wait till you hear! I really shouldn't brag, I know, but the effect of my article has been colossal, truly colossal! It seems that when the young man's fiancée found out about his betrayal of the girl, she was so angry she called the wedding off, understand?

LUDOVICO: Really?

ALFREDO: And that isn't all! Not only is the wedding off, but the young man himself is overcome with remorse! The way I wrote the story up and the part about the girl's attempted suicide has apparently hit home. He's out of his mind!

LUDOVICO: You mean the naval lieutenant?

ALFREDO: That's the one. His name is—wait—Laspiga, I think. Completely lost his head. So the consul says.

LUDOVICO: And how does he know?

ALFREDO: Because the father of the bride apparently looked him up and told him so.

LUDOVICO: What a mess!

ALFREDO: Exactly. That's what I was trying to tell you, now that you're involved in it.

LUDOVICO: I?

ALFREDO: All of us, my dear sir. Look at me, probably with a libel suit on my hands!

LUDOVICO: But what about the bride's father?

ALFREDO: He's raising hell! Because his daughter was only angry, at first, but then—well, you understand—practically on her wedding night—tears, convulsions, hysterics—oh, it's a mess, all right! Well, since it was the consul who met Laspiga in Smyrna and introduced him to Miss Drei, naturally—

LUDOVICO:—the father went to *him* for information?

ALFREDO: So it seems.

LUDOVICO: And I can just imagine what he told him! They even blame her for the death of the child!

(At this point Franco Laspiga bursts into the room. He is very nervous and excited, with the pale, tortured face of a man who hasn't slept for days and is nearly out of his mind. He is twenty-seven years old, blond, tall, slender, elegantly dressed.)

FRANCO: Excuse me! Please!—Ersilia— Where is she? Where is she? Is she here? Where is she?

LUDOVICO *(surprised)*: She's— Who are you?

FRANCO: I'm Franco Laspiga. The one for whom—

ALFREDO: Ah, so you're Laspiga! We were just talking about you!

LUDOVICO: You here, too?

FRANCO: I went to the hospital—she'd gone! Then I went to the newspaper and they told me— *(He breaks off and turns to Alfredo.)* I beg your pardon. Are you the writer, Ludovico Nota?

ALFREDO: I? No. That's him!

FRANCO *(to Ludovico)*: You're Nota?

LUDOVICO: Yes. Good God, what is this? Does everybody know?

ALFREDO: Ah, Mr. Nota, you forget who you are.

LUDOVICO *(very annoyed, raising his arms)*: Well, I give up!

ALFREDO: Your noble deed has made quite an impression, it seems!

FRANCO *(confused, upset)*: Deed? What deed? For God's sake, tell me! Isn't she here?

LUDOVICO *(angrily, to Alfredo)*: It wasn't exactly my idea to put her on display, or to make a public spectacle of myself, either!

ALFREDO: Of course not. What do you mean by that?

LUDOVICO *(furious)*: I mean that I'm sick of this whole wretched business! *(To Franco:)* You can take my word for it, the young lady has only been here about an hour.

FRANCO: Then she *is* here! Where?

LUDOVICO: I went to pick her up at the hospital. She had no place to go and I offered to put her up for a few days. Naturally, I was planning to move to a hotel this evening.

FRANCO: I'm so grateful to you—

LUDOVICO *(exploding, at the height of his exasperation)*: Why grateful? Why? Because I'm no longer young? Is that why you're grateful? What do you want here?

FRANCO *(immediately, heatedly)*: Want? I want to redeem myself, sir—to throw myself at her feet, to beg her forgiveness!

ALFREDO: Good for you! That's the way to talk!

LUDOVICO: You might have thought of that a little sooner.

FRANCO: You're right, of course. I never realized . . . I tried, I tried to forget it . . . I passed whole days in— But where is she? In there? Let me see her!

LUDOVICO: Not right now. I don't want her to—

FRANCO: I have to talk to her! Please!

ALFREDO: Perhaps we'd better tell her you're here first.

LUDOVICO: She's in bed.

ALFREDO: Because the excitement—

FRANCO: She's still sick?

LUDOVICO: She fainted in here a few minutes ago.

ALFREDO: And her joy at seeing you, you know, might upset—

FRANCO *(almost raving)*: I never thought, I never believed

that dream . . . My God, that it could come to this! A blow to shatter my whole life, destroy everything . . . All those newsboys, shouting out the headlines . . . I felt as if someone had picked me up and hurled me to the ground . . . Everybody shouting, shouting–my fiancée, her father, her mother, all the neighbors, up and down the stairs . . . I ran at once to the hospital . . . They wouldn't let me see her . . . The harm, the harm I've done everybody! The whole world is full of the harm I've done! I have to make it up to her! Don't you see? I have to make it up to her!

ALFREDO: Of course, of course you do! And you will, I'm sure of it! It's the only way! And we're all delighted! *(Onoria enters from the bedroom signaling them to be quiet. Then she closes the door behind her and comes forward.)*

ONORIA: Not so loud! Not so loud! Please! She heard everything!

FRANCO: She knows I'm here?

ONORIA: Yes, that's just it. And she's all worked up about it. She says she'll throw herself out the window if you go in there!

FRANCO: What? But why?

ALFREDO *(simultaneously)*: What? How can that be?

ONORIA: That child is an angel! She says she doesn't want it!

LUDOVICO: Doesn't want what?

ONORIA *(to Franco)*: She says you must go back to your fiancée.

FRANCO *(promptly and firmly)*: No! That's all over! That's all over now!

ONORIA: She doesn't want anyone else to be hurt because of her.

FRANCO: But she's the one who was hurt the most! She's the one I'm engaged to now!

ONORIA: She won't even discuss it.

FRANCO: But I came here to beg her forgiveness, to make it up to her for all the wrong I've done!

ONORIA: Please! Keep your voice down! Don't let her hear you!

FRANCO *(to Ludovico)*: You tell her! You persuade her!

LUDOVICO: I'll try. It seems only right, after all.

FRANCO: Tell her not to worry, that I'm here because of her, that my first duty is to her, and that she mustn't do anything to spoil this last chance we have to settle everything together! Tell her that! Please!

(Ludovico exits into the bedroom.)

ONORIA *(obstinately)*: It's because of your fiancée.

FRANCO *(annoyed)*: But I tell you it's all over with her! All finished!

ONORIA: She'll never agree to it.

FRANCO: But why? I can't give up now! For my own sake, I can't! Because it's all come back to me—the way it was between us.

ALFREDO: Ah, the re-evocation of the past! So you remember now!

FRANCO: A time that—I don't know why—a time that seemed so distant to me, so far away! As if I'd dreamed it all! So that it was as if, I don't know, as if none of it had actually happened—that night, the promise I made her . . . the promises you make because . . . yes, because, at the time, you *have* to make them, you *want* to make them—

ALFREDO: And then you forget . . .

FRANCO *(excited, pouring it out)*: I thought, I thought it didn't matter, that I could forget about it, in spite of the letters I used to get from her, letters I just threw away, unable to take them seriously. It's incredible, incredible that I could lie, lie to myself like that, do what I've done —while she believed in my promise—it was all real, all real to her and not just a dream, as it was for me! So real that my betrayal was—yes, now I understand—was for her as for me, once I felt the full force of it in all those voices shouting at me, the blow—the hard reality that takes you unawares, that crushes, that annihilates you!

(Ludovico returns. He is disturbed, very serious and determined.)

LUDOVICO: It's no use. No. For the moment, it's impossible.

FRANCO: What do you mean, impossible? What did she say? What did she say?

LUDOVICO: I made her promise to see you tomorrow.

FRANCO: Please, I can't stand another night of it! I'll go mad!

LUDOVICO: I tell you, it's impossible. She can't see you now.

FRANCO: I haven't slept for days! Just let me have a word with her! Please!

LUDOVICO *(firmly, almost harshly)*: It's useless to insist. *(More kindly.)* It would only make things worse for you, believe me.

FRANCO: But why?

LUDOVICO: Give her a night to think things over. I talked to her. I told her—

FRANCO: Why won't she have me? If she's worried about my fianceé, she can forget about her! It's all over! I don't understand. Didn't she try to kill herself over me? Then why won't she even see me?

LUDOVICO *(losing his patience)*: She will! She will! But for God's sake give her time to calm down a bit!

ALFREDO: And you must try to get hold of yourself, too.

FRANCO: I can't . . . I can't . . .

LUDOVICO *(more kindly)*: Listen: I'm sure she'll change her mind tomorrow. I'm sure of it. *(To Onoria:)* Meanwhile, you go in to her, please. Don't leave her alone.

ONORIA *(hurrying toward the bedroom)*: Yes, of course.

Turn on the lights. It's getting dark in here. *(She exits.)* *(Ludovico turns on the lights.)*

LUDOVICO: I think we'd all better go now.

FRANCO: Can't I even look in at her?

LUDOVICO: You'll see her and talk to her in the morning. Now let's go. *(He indicates the door.)*

ALFREDO: She'll come around, you'll see. It's the only way.

LUDOVICO *(following them out)*: Right now she needs rest. She's upset and very nervous. Come.

FRANCO: I thought my coming here would . . .

LUDOVICO *(to Alfredo, urging them out)*: Please . . .

ALFREDO: Thank you. *(He exits.)*

LUDOVICO *(to Franco)*: After you. *(As they exit.)* Well, you see . . . *(They shut the door behind them.)*

(The stage remains empty for a moment. Street noises are heard. Then the bedroom door opens and Ersilia enters, followed by Onoria. The girl is very nervous and in the act of dressing herself. The following scene must be played in great excitement.)

ERSILIA: No, no, I have to get out of here! I have to get out of here!

ONORIA: But where? Where are you going?

ERSILIA: I don't know! But I have to go!

ONORIA: It's insane!

ERSILIA: To disappear, down there, in the street! Anywhere! *(Starts to put on her hat.)*

ONORIA *(holding her back)*: No, no! I can't let you do this!

ERSILIA: Leave me alone! Leave me alone! I can't stay here!

ONORIA: But why?

ERSILIA: Because I don't want to listen to anyone any more! I don't want to see anyone!

ONORIA: Then you won't see him, that's all!

ERSILIA: Not just him! Anyone! Let me go, please!

ONORIA: All right, no one! I'll tell Mr. Nota myself. I promise you!

ERSILIA: Is it my fault they wouldn't let me die?

ONORIA: Your fault? What do you mean?

ERSILIA: They all blame me! They all accuse me!

ONORIA: Of course not! Who does?

ERSILIA: All of them! Everyone! Didn't you hear?

ONORIA: He only came here to make amends, to be forgiven.

ERSILIA: Forgiven! I only talked about him because I thought I was dying! But I've had enough now! I've had enough!

ONORIA: All right! You've had enough! Tomorrow I'll tell Mr. Nota—

ERSILIA: I thought I could stay here in peace.

ONORIA: Why can't you?

ERSILIA: Because they'll keep after him, they'll wear him down! You'll see!

ONORIA: Who? Mr. Nota?

ERSILIA: Yes.

ONORIA: No. I don't think so. He's a little strange, but at heart he's a good man, Mr. Nota.

ERSILIA: But there's the other one—that other one—

ONORIA: Who?

ERSILIA: The man I didn't even want to mention! He's threatening to sue the paper!

ONORIA: The consul?

ERSILIA: Yes. He'll never leave me alone, never! *(A new outburst.)* Oh, God! Oh, God! Let me go! Let me go!

ONORIA: No, no! You just keep calm now! Don't worry! Mr. Nota will know how to handle him! What can he do anyway? After the way he treated you! There, now! Just calm down! Everything will be all right.

(Ersilia collapses into a chair.)

You see? You shouldn't even be up.

ERSILIA *(desperately)*: You're right, you're right. Oh, what should I do?

ONORIA: Well, now, you just get back in bed and get some rest. I'll bring you something to eat, and then you try and sleep.

ERSILIA *(softly, timidly, confiding in her as one woman to another)*: But you see, I'm . . . I'm just the way I am and . . .

ONORIA: And?

ERSILIA: I mean, I haven't a thing, not a thing, with me. At the hotel I had an overnight bag . . . I don't know where it is. Maybe the police took it.

ONORIA: We'll pick it up tomorrow. Don't you worry about it. I'll send someone or go myself.

ERSILIA: Yes, but right now . . . right now . . . I'm naked.

ONORIA *(affectionately, comfortingly)*: I'll take care of that. I'll take care of everything! You get back in bed and stop worrying. Go on now. I'll be right back. Go on. *(Onoria exits.)*

(Ersilia remains seated and stares about the room in bewilderment. Then, desperately tired, she rests her head against the back of the chair. But she has difficulty breathing and passes a hand over her cold forehead. Afraid of fainting again, she rises and opens a window. With evening, the street noises have become fainter and less violent, then almost nonexistent. After a moment or two, however, a group of young men, laughing and joking, come down the street. One of them is singing a popular song in a loud, raucous voice. Finally, he cracks a note and stops, amid the jeers and shouts of his friends. Ersilia, who has gone to sit down by the table, waits for the revelers to pass, then looks about again with wide, staring eyes.)

ERSILIA *(murmuring, almost inaudibly)*: The street . . .

CURTAIN

ACT II

Ludovico Nota's apartment, the following morning.

The curtain rises on an empty stage, then the outside door opens and Emma, the maid, ushers in Ludovico and Franco Laspiga.

LUDOVICO *(to Emma)*: Mrs. Onoria?

EMMA *(indicating the bedroom door)*: She's in there, with the young lady.

LUDOVICO: How is Miss Drei?

EMMA: Not too good, sir. She was sick most of the night. I don't think either of them got a wink of sleep.

FRANCO: If only I could have talked to her last night!

LUDOVICO *(to Emma)*: Go in there very quietly and tell Mrs. Onoria we're here.

EMMA: Yes, sir. *(She starts for the bedroom.)*

LUDOVICO: Is there any mail?

EMMA: Yes, sir. Over there, on the desk. *(She opens the bedroom door very softly and exits.)*

LUDOVICO *(to Franco, as he goes toward the desk)*: Sit down, sit down.

FRANCO: No, thank you. I can't.

LUDOVICO: Lord, it's stuffy in here! *(He opens a window and begins to glance through his mail. The street noises now include the bustling sounds of an open-air market. Suddenly annoyed, he shuts the window and goes over to Franco with a newspaper item that has caught his attention.)* Look at this! Read here! *(He gives Franco the newspaper.)*

FRANCO *(reading the item)*: A retraction?

LUDOVICO: Yes. It says they'll publish it tomorrow.

(Onoria enters from the bedroom, followed by Emma, who promptly exits out the other door.)

FRANCO *(anxiously, seeing her enter)*: Ah, at last . . .

ONORIA *(waving her hands about)*: What a night! What a night!

FRANCO: What's she doing? Isn't she coming out?

ONORIA: If she can. She knows you're here. But please don't upset her. She dozed off a bit this morning.

LUDOVICO: I suppose this racket outside–

ONORIA: No, she woke up when Emma came in to tell us you were here. I was so afraid she'd refuse to see you again, like last night.

FRANCO: No!

ONORIA: But now she says she does want to talk to you.

FRANCO: Thank God! She must have changed her mind!

LUDOVICO: Of course she has. And if she hasn't, we'll change it for her. You'll see.

ONORIA: I'm not so sure. Last night, after you left, she tried to run away.

LUDOVICO: Run away?

FRANCO: Where to? Why?

ONORIA: Who knows? She just had to get away, she said. I had a terrible time keeping her from doing it. I can't understand how they could let her out of that hospital. She's not at all well yet.

LUDOVICO *(a little annoyed, coldly)*: Well, she was all right when she was with me.

ONORIA: Of course she wasn't! It was all she could do to stay on her feet, to pretend she wasn't in pain. She's so afraid you'll become tired of her.

LUDOVICO: I? But it isn't . . . I mean, it's really up to . . . *(He indicates Franco.)*

FRANCO: Yes, of course! I'll take care of her! I'll make sure she's all right!

ONORIA: I'm going to lie down for a while. I simply can't keep my eyes open. But if you need me—

LUDOVICO: No, go ahead, go ahead.

ONORIA: —don't hesitate to call me. *(She starts for the door, then turns back to Ludovico.)* Oh, I meant to tell you! The child hasn't a thing with her. They took her bag; it's either at the hotel or the police have it. Someone ought to go and get it.

LUDOVICO: Yes, yes, we'll take care of all that.

ONORIA: But right away, this morning. She's— *(She was about to say "naked," but she stops in time.)* Well, a girl always has to look her best, you know! You will take care of it?

FRANCO: I'll go myself!

ONORIA: Perhaps it would be better if you went, Mr. Nota.

LUDOVICO *(impatiently)*: All right, all right! *(More calmly, referring to Ersilia:)* First, let's hear what she has to say.

ONORIA: Please—be nice to her.

LUDOVICO *(sharply)*: Well, I like that! You telling me to be nice to her, when only yesterday—

ONORIA: But I had no idea! You know, she's like one of those mangy little dogs you see in the streets with all the other dogs after it! The weaker, the more helpless it is, the more the others worry and torment it. She's so discouraged, so defeated, the poor thing!

LUDOVICO: Anyway, there have been a lot of changes since yesterday, it seems.

ONORIA: What? Anything to do with her?

LUDOVICO: Everything! I thought this whole business was over and done with, and I find just the opposite! Things couldn't be worse! First, that reporter and his story, then this gentleman. And finally, that damned consul making trouble all over the place. *(To Franco:)* You saw the paper.

FRANCO: You mean Grotti is here?

LUDOVICO *(heatedly)*: Of course he's here! Grotti and everybody else! And apparently your prospective father-in-law went to see him!

FRANCO *(stunned, disturbed)*: He did? What for?

LUDOVICO: How should I know? For information, probably.

FRANCO *(indignantly)*: What can her family still expect from me? After slamming the door in my face! So Grotti, too, has turned against her!

ONORIA: They all have.

LUDOVICO: So it seems. In fact, there's no doubt about it. Now you understand, I'm a writer, I lead a quiet life . . .

FRANCO *(almost to himself, angrily)*: What I'd like to know is why this man, Grotti–

LUDOVICO: Ask him, why don't you? As for me, I only became involved, you see, because the girl's story interested me. I mean, as a story, as a slice of life–the events, the people–as I imagined them, naturally. But now this whole mess, one thing after another, well–I mean, it's completely spoiled it, it's spoiled everything. Anyway, it's lucky you're here now.

FRANCO: Yes, I'm here! I'm here!

ONORIA: Well, I'll go downstairs. *(With a warning gesture.)* Be careful! *(She exits.)*

FRANCO *(determined, energetically)*: I'll take her away from here. It will be easy, with my connections. Yes, far away from here!

LUDOVICO: Go slowly. Don't lose your head again. You see what can happen.

FRANCO: Slowly? And what about Ersilia?

LUDOVICO: She's the most tragic example of what I mean: the victim of this whole affair.

FRANCO: Yes, but do you know why? Because I didn't lose

my head, as you put it, because I did the sensible thing instead. And so I betrayed her, and myself as well! I left the sea—the sea!—to smother here, in this swamp of everyday living.

LUDOVICO: Well, you know, there does come a time in everyone's life—

FRANCO *(increasingly impetuous)*: No! No! It's only when you allow yourself to think the life you dreamed of is impossible that what seemed so easy, so easy that you could reach out and touch it, suddenly becomes difficult, unattainable.

LUDOVICO: There are times, I know, when our spirits free themselves of humdrum considerations.

FRANCO: Yes, that's what I meant!

LUDOVICO: When we rise above the petty obstacles of daily life, ignore our little wants, shake off our mean little cares and mediocre obligations.

FRANCO: Exactly! And so, free at last, we can breathe in an atmosphere where everything becomes possible, where even the most difficult things become easy.

LUDOVICO: And everything falls into place, everything goes smoothly, as if divinely inspired. Yes, I know. But these are only moments, my dear boy.

FRANCO *(vehemently)*: Because we give in, because we don't hang on to them, that's why!

LUDOVICO *(smiling sadly)*: No, no. It's because we have no idea what lovely tricks and jokes, what nice surprises are in store for us as we soar with our heads above the clouds, breathing in the heady air of those moments—moments when, free of all restraints, all rationalizations, we are dazzled by the flaming glory of our own dreams and notice nothing else. But one day, Laspiga, one terrible day, our feet strike solid ground again.

FRANCO: Yes, it's true, but that's the point! You mustn't give in! You mustn't let it happen! That's why I told you I want to take her away, far away—back to where she waited for me, where she was so happy and trusted in her dream. It was a dream I had shared and then dismissed as a kind of madness. As if I'd given some proof of extraordinary wisdom and self-control. Well, that's all over with! I've found my real self again, and I owe it all to her!

LUDOVICO: Don't set your hopes too high. She's not the same girl.

FRANCO: I'll soon put her on her feet again! You'll see! *(The bedroom door opens and Ersilia appears.)* Here she is! *(At sight of her, softly:)* Good God! *(Ersilia enters and goes toward Ludovico. Her appearance is dishevelled, her hair uncombed, her face very pale. She is desperately determined.)*

ERSILIA: I can't do it, Mr. Nota! I shouldn't even have come here. Your offer . . . No, it's impossible! I can't do it! I can't!

LUDOVICO: What are you talking about? Look who's here! *(He indicates Franco.)*

FRANCO: Ersilia! Ersilia!

ERSILIA: You . . . What do you want? Don't you see who I am? What I am?

FRANCO *(emotionally, approaching her)*: I see what's happened to you, but you're still my Ersilia! My Ersilia! *(He starts to embrace her.)*

ERSILIA *(horrified, backing away from him)*: Don't touch me! Don't touch me! Leave me alone!

FRANCO: What? You can say that to me? Don't you realize you're still mine, mine, just as always?

ERSILIA: Oh, this is unbearable! What can I say, how can I make you understand that it's all over?

FRANCO: All over? How can it be all over, now that I've come back to you?

ERSILIA: What you once meant to me—it can never be the same.

FRANCO: But it can! It can! Because I haven't changed! I'm just the same!

ERSILIA: And what about me? My God, use your eyes! I can't ever be the same again! I don't want you!

FRANCO: But that isn't so! You tried to kill yourself over me! You said so yourself! Well?

ERSILIA *(darkly, desperately resolved)*: Well, then—it isn't true!

FRANCO: It isn't true?

ERSILIA: No. Not because of you. I didn't even come to see you when I got back . . . I lied!

FRANCO: You lied?

ERSILIA: Yes. I gave a reason—a reason that in that particular moment happened to be true. But it isn't true now.

FRANCO: It isn't? Why isn't it?

ERSILIA: Because, unfortunately, I'm alive, still alive.

FRANCO: Unfortunately? It's a miracle!

ERSILIA: Oh, yes. A miracle. So you can condemn me to be the very person I tried to kill? No! No, that's enough of her! The person who spoke that way is gone, and what she said no longer holds—for either of us. That's all.

LUDOVICO: But why?

FRANCO: If that was the reason you wanted to kill yourself . . .

ERSILIA: Exactly! To kill myself! To put an end to it! I'm dead! Everything's changed!

FRANCO: As if I couldn't make it up to you . . . I can!

ERSILIA: No. I don't want that.

FRANCO: Why not? If you tried to kill yourself over me, then now you ought to have all the more reason to live!

LUDOVICO: He's right!

FRANCO: That's why I'm here!

ERSILIA *(suddenly changing tone, sharply, accentuating every syllable and emphasizing each word with abrupt, definite gestures of her hands)*: It's all I can do even to recognize you!

FRANCO *(stunned)*: You—me?

(Ersilia gestures impatiently, helplessly, and turns away from them to sit down. A pause. The men look at her the way you look at someone who unexpectedly reveals himself to be entirely different from what you first imagined.)

ERSILIA: Don't push me too far. *(Another pause, then resuming her former manner.)* Admit it. You don't recognize me either.

FRANCO *(subdued, hurt)*: That's not true. Is that the way it really is with you?

ERSILIA: Oh, so completely that, you know, if I'd seen you last night, it would have been impossible to say, really . . .

FRANCO: What?

ERSILIA: That I killed myself over you. I couldn't have!—Not even your voice . . . your eyes . . . Is that really your voice? Are those your eyes? I saw you . . . Who knows now what you looked like?

FRANCO *(coldly)*: You're driving me away, Ersilia. You —you make me doubt myself—and you.

ERSILIA: Because you don't know, you can't understand the horror of a life suddenly restored to you, like this . . . like . . . like a memory which, instead of remaining locked safely away within you, suddenly appears . . . appears unexpectedly before your eyes . . . so changed you can barely recognize it. You can no longer see yourself in this memory because you, too, have changed and the life you are confronted with no longer has anything to do with you, even though you know it was once yours, the way, perhaps, you once were—the way you talked, the way you looked, the way you moved. But as reflected in someone else's eyes, not your own.

FRANCO: But I'm that someone else, Ersilia! I'm the man in that memory, just the way I was!

ERSILIA: You can't be! My God, don't you understand? Because now, as I look at you, I'm certain you were never that man!

FRANCO: Never?

ERSILIA: Why look surprised? Do you think I didn't notice just now, as we were talking, that you had the same impression of me?

FRANCO: Yes, you're right. But why say such things now, things that—

ERSILIA: Because they're true! Why not profit by them? Everybody else does. I'm the only one who can't!—You're not to blame, Franco.

FRANCO: Not to blame? What do you mean?

ERSILIA: For what you did to me.

FRANCO: Why aren't I? That's why I'm here!

ERSILIA: In life—oh, yes—in life these things just happen. Anyone can make them happen.

FRANCO: Yes, but afterward you're sorry, as sorry as I am now. I'm here because I'm really sorry, you know, not simply out of a sense of duty.

ERSILIA: But if you find out I'm not what you thought I was, not the person you imagined . . .

FRANCO *(in despair)*: Oh, my God, what are you saying?

ERSILIA: You, too, Mr. Nota—I'm not what you thought. But I swear to you I would have given anything, anything to be the girl you saw in your novel! For you, yes, for you I might have succeeded, because I would have found a new life in your art. But you see, this other life, the life I tried to get rid of, won't leave me alone. It has me in its teeth and it won't let go! They're all still here, all around me. Where am I to go?

LUDOVICO *(quietly, to Franco)*: I told you. You'll have to give her time. She needs rest and–

ERSILIA: Even you've turned against me now?

LUDOVICO: Against you? On the contrary!

ERSILIA: But you know, you know it's impossible!

LUDOVICO: Impossible? I wouldn't say that.

ERSILIA: Oh, I can see it means nothing to you! You only guessed it all, only imagined everything, and it made you happy to find out you were right! But what you only imagined I actually suffered in my living flesh– the shame, the horror!

LUDOVICO: You mean–

ERSILIA: Tell him! Tell him what I did that night, so he'll go away!

LUDOVICO: I will not! No one can blame you for that!

ERSILIA: Then I'll tell him! *(To Franco:)* Do you know I offered myself in the street to the first man who'd have me?

LUDOVICO *(quickly, heatedly, as Franco hides his face in his hands)*: She was desperate! On the verge of suicide! Do you understand?

FRANCO: Yes, yes! Oh, Ersilia!

LUDOVICO: The next morning she took the poison. She didn't even have enough money to pay her hotel bill. Understand?

FRANCO: Of course! And this only makes it worse for me, makes my responsibility for what happened all the greater!

ERSILIA *(in despair, shouting)*: No! It wasn't you!

FRANCO: It was! It was! Who else then?

ERSILIA *(at the end of her patience)*: You want to make me tell everything? Everything? The things you don't admit even to yourself? *(She pauses a moment to gain control of herself, then speaks firmly, coldly, staring into space with the eyes of a lunatic.)* That morning I coldly estimated the disgust I felt, to find out whether I could stand it. I had some of the poison in my purse, more of it in my suitcase. A disinfectant I used in the baby's room. Before leaving the hotel, I looked at myself in the mirror over the bureau. *(To Ludovico:)* Exactly as you envisioned it, you see. *(As before.)* And then I powdered my face and put make-up on, just as I had the night before. Yes, and later, sitting there in the park, I didn't know, I didn't want to know I'd actually go through with it. Not until the moment I opened my bag and felt the bottle in my hand. I could just as easily not have done it, if things had happened differently—if somebody else had come along who wanted me or whom I wanted. I really don't know whether I would have killed myself. Probably not. I *had* powdered my face, I *had* put lipstick on. And I was wearing my best dress . . . *(She leaps to her feet.)* And what about my being here? What do you think that means? It means I mastered my disgust, after having measured it against the only alternative—death! Otherwise I wouldn't be here, living with a man who doesn't know me, who only wrote me a letter and offered to take me in!

FRANCO *(with sudden determination)*: Listen! I know, I know why you're saying all this, why you feel you have to torture yourself.

ERSILIA *(violently)*: Torture myself? It's you who are torturing me!

FRANCO: Ah, you see? You admit it! You really feel we're all being cruel to you! Then why won't you let one of us make amends for his cruelty?

ERSILIA: How? By inflicting it on me all over again?

FRANCO: Of course not!

ERSILIA *(hammering out each word)*: I told you I was pretending, I told you it wasn't true, I told you I was lying, and I tell you again! No one else is to blame! It wasn't your fault! It was life, that's all. This life that clings to me still. God, what can I do? I've tried, I've tried, but I've never been able to make it mean anything! What else can I say to make you go away?

(There is a loud knocking at the door.)

LUDOVICO: Who is it? Come in.

(The door opens and Emma appears.)

What do you want?

EMMA: There's a Mr. Grotti here.

ERSILIA *(with a cry)*: At last! I knew he'd come!

LUDOVICO: He wants to talk to me?

FRANCO: I'll see him!

EMMA: No. He wishes to see the young lady.

ERSILIA: Yes, yes, let me talk to him! Let me talk to him, please! *(To Emma:)* Show him in!

(Emma leaves.)

I must, I must talk to him. The sooner the better!

(Grotti enters. He is a dark, solid-looking man in his late thirties. He is dressed in black, and his eyes, his whole face reflect a hard, somber reserve.)

Come in, Mr. Grotti! *(To Ludovico:)* The Consul Grotti. *(To Grotti:)* Mr. Ludovico Nota.

GROTTI *(bowing)*: I know who you are, of course.

ERSILIA: Who was so kind as to invite me here. *(Indicating Franco.)* Mr. Laspiga you already know.

FRANCO: Oh, yes, under quite different circumstances! But now I've come back–

ERSILIA *(immediately interrupting)*: Please–

FRANCO: No! *(To Grotti:)* Look at her! *(Indicating Ersilia.)* Her state of mind, the condition she's in are good enough reasons to explain my presence here.

ERSILIA *(exasperated)*: Leave my condition out of it! I've told you over and over there's no reason for you to be here! I'll say it again in front of him, so he'll know that I'm upset only because I can't seem to make you understand this!

FRANCO: Yes, you like to keep telling me that, don't you? Because you know that my fiancée's father went to see him, didn't you?

ERSILIA *(shocked)*: No. I didn't know that. *(Violently upset, but doing her best to control herself, she turns to stare at Grotti.)* And . . . and you . . . you told him about me?

GROTTI *(coldly, composed)*: No, Miss Drei. I only promised him I'd come and talk to you.

FRANCO *(immediately, vehemently)*: Ah, it won't do any good, you know!

ERSILIA *(imperiously, scornfully)*: I'd like to talk to Mr. Grotti alone! *(Then gently, to Ludovico:)* Please, Mr. Nota.

LUDOVICO: Oh, as far as I'm concerned– *(He starts for the door.)*

FRANCO: No, no! Wait! *(To Ersilia, stiffly proud:)* I'm going now. *(Turning to Grotti:)* But first I want to tell you, Mr. Grotti, so you can pass the information on, that it's useless, absolutely useless, because it's not up to her to decide, but up to me! *(To Ersilia:)* Up to now I've begged you, I've pleaded with you, and I've submitted to hearing you say the worst, the most abominable things to me. But I've had enough! Now you're going to listen to me! Yes, you're free to send me away, but this doesn't mean that I have to return to a woman who, like everybody else who read your terrible story, was shocked and horrified by my conduct and quite rightly slammed the door in my face! Am I supposed to go back to her, now that she's changed her mind and sent somebody here to plead for her?

GROTTI: You're wrong, Laspiga. I'm not here for that.

ERSILIA: And I've already told you that your conduct had nothing to do with my suicide attempt!

FRANCO: That's not true!

ERSILIA: Not true? Mr. Nota was right here when I–

FRANCO: Oh, yes, that's what you said, all right! *(To Grotti:)* She said the most horrible things about herself, things no one should admit, ever! *(To Ersilia:)* But I have my conscience, even if, because of what I did to you, you now feel compelled to send me away. And no matter what he tells you or what you say to him, no matter what you both decide I should do, I'm not going to change my mind! *(To Ludovico:)* And now let's go, sir. I know you're on my side and that you approve. Good-by, Mr. Grotti. *(He starts for the door.)*

GROTTI *(nodding)*: Good-by, Laspiga.

LUDOVICO *(who has gone up to Ersilia, softly, comfortingly)*: Meanwhile, I'll see about your suitcase. I hope to have it for you very soon.

ERSILIA *(moved)*: Yes, thank you. And please forgive me.

LUDOVICO: There's nothing to forgive. *(To Grotti:)* I'll leave you now.

GROTTI: Thank you.

(Ludovico and Franco exit.)

(No sooner have they gone than Ersilia begins to tremble and seems to shrink away from Grotti, looking askance at him out of frightened eyes. Grotti wheels about and transfixes her with a furiously scornful and penetrating stare. Unable to resist this look, Ersilia hides her face in her hands and hunches her shoulders, almost crouching, as if steeling herself to bear the full weight of his fury. Grotti then slowly, threateningly approaches her. Softly, hissing the words through clenched teeth:)

Fool! Fool! Such childish lies!

ERSILIA *(terrified, an arm raised in self-defense)*: I really did try to kill myself!

GROTTI *(railing at her)*: And why? Why, why, why? So you could drown us in your lies?

ERSILIA: No! I didn't want that! Didn't you hear? He says his decision to come here had nothing to do with me. And I shouted it to his face! I swear I did! I told him over and over that I lied when I said I'd done it for his sake!

GROTTI: But he doesn't believe it! Can't you see he doesn't believe it?

ERSILIA *(reacting scornfully)*: Is that my fault? He's too ashamed to believe it, that's why!

GROTTI *(contemptuously)*: Ashamed? You dare to mention that word? You?

ERSILIA: Why not? Am I the only one who ought to feel that way? The only one? You're wrong! I have less reason to be ashamed than any of you! Oh, yes! I know! You won't face that, because at least I had the courage to kill myself! Oh, yes! That much I could do! But not you!

GROTTI: I? Kill myself?

ERSILIA: Oh, never mind about that! Anyway, shame, remorse—that wasn't what made me do it. You can bear your guilt. You have money, a position. But I—I found myself in the street. Alone. Naked. And then, you know, it's hard . . . . it's unbearable! I was desperate—I kept thinking of the baby—and then that final degradation. That's why I did it!

GROTTI: But even then you couldn't help lying, could you?

ERSILIA: I didn't mean to. It just came out. But it's true that he promised to marry me.

GROTTI: He was only flirting with you.

ERSILIA: That's not so! But even if it were, then he's doubly to blame! Because when he came back here and got himself engaged to somebody else, he didn't know what was going on between you and me.

GROTTI: But you! You knew what was going on between us. And still you lied!

ERSILIA: Wasn't what he did much worse? He had no idea what I was up to, but he was calmly prepared to forget all about me and marry somebody else.

GROTTI: It only proves what I said, that he was just flirting with you.

ERSILIA: That's not true! He said so himself! And he wouldn't be behaving like this now if it were! But you like to think that, because it makes it easy for you, because it gives you an excuse for what you did to me behind his back the moment he'd gone!

GROTTI: And you made all this trouble here to prevent him from marrying somebody else?

ERSILIA: No. It never occurred to me. I said what I said when I thought I was dying. I didn't try to stop anything! And I'm not trying now! I'm not!

GROTTI: Suppose he hadn't betrayed you? Suppose you'd found him here, ready to keep his promise?

ERSILIA *(horrified)*: No, no! Never! I wouldn't have deceived him! I swear I wouldn't! I didn't even try to find him—he can tell you that himself! And it was because he betrayed me, really betrayed me, that I was able to lie, to say that I killed myself for him.

GROTTI: You didn't try to find him?

ERSILIA: No.

GROTTI: Then how did you know he was getting married?

ERSILIA: Oh, yes . . . I—I did go there . . . to the Navy Department . . .

GROTTI: You see? You did look for him.

ERSILIA *(threateningly, doing her best to control her mounting rage)*: You ought to thank me!

GROTTI: For what? For trying to find him?

ERSILIA: No! For having no desire to revenge myself when I found out he'd left the service and what he'd done to me. You think you've caught me in another lie, that as I walked up the stairs of that office building I did intend to deceive him. But you don't know how I felt when I climbed those stairs. I was alone, lost, that terrible scene branded forever in my memory—that horrible moment when your wife caught us together—with the screams of the people who found the baby's body ringing in my ears—so vivid, so clear . . . I was in despair . . . like a beggar, a derelict with no way out except in death or madness. And like a maniac, I was going to tell him everything, everything!

GROTTI: About us?

ERSILIA: No! About you! About what you did after he left, how you took advantage—

GROTTI: It was all my doing?

ERSILIA: Yes! You knew the way I was after he'd gone! Oh, I warn you! There's nothing I can't say now, nothing—the things no one ever dares to say—I've touched bottom, the very bottom—I'll shout them all out, the truths of madmen—the horrible things you can only scream in the darkness—when everything is gone and shame is meaningless! You took me when I was helpless, burning from the fire he lit in my flesh, still hot from his touch and wanting more! Go ahead, deny it! Tell me I didn't bite you! Tell me I didn't scratch your neck, your arms, your hands!

GROTTI: You bitch! You were just leading me on!

ERSILIA: Liar! Liar! Never! It was you!

GROTTI: At first, yes! But afterward?

ERSILIA: Never! Never!

GROTTI: You used to squeeze my arm when you thought no one was looking!

ERSILIA: It's not true!

GROTTI: Not true? Liar! Once you even sneaked up behind me and pricked my shoulder with a needle!

ERSILIA: Because you wouldn't let me alone!

GROTTI: A fine excuse!

ERSILIA: I was only a servant!

GROTTI: And so you had to submit to me, is that it?

ERSILIA: My body, my body submitted! My heart, never! Never! I hated you!

GROTTI: But you wanted me! Oh, how you wanted me!

ERSILIA: And I hated you for it! Yes, the more I wanted you, the more I loathed you! Afterward, I could have torn you apart, the way I was torn by my own shame and disgust! My heart never gave in to you! I used to lie there, afterward, bleeding inside at the thought of what I was doing to myself! I used to stare at my bare arms and bite them in my frenzy! I gave in to you, I always gave in to you, but my heart no, never! And your lust stripped my life of its only happiness—a happiness I almost couldn't believe in—the joy of thinking I was going to be married—

GROTTI: —while all the time he was back here, getting ready to marry someone else.

ERSILIA: So you see? We're all scum! How can you stand there and blame it all on me? Is it my fault that I've never been strong enough to make anything of my life? . . . My God, nothing, ever . . . not even, I don't know, not even something fragile, something so fragile that, if you dropped it, it would smash into a thousand pieces. But then at least you'd know, you'd know by all those broken fragments that you once had something. . . . My whole life . . . one day after another . . . and no one I could ever call my own. . . . At the mercy of every chance event, of every whim . . . never left alone long enough even to take a deep breath . . . pushed and pulled this way and that . . . used and thrown away . . . and never a moment, never a time when I could look up and say, "Wait! I'm also here!" *(Suddenly turning on him like a whipped animal.)* And now what do you want from me? Why are you here?

GROTTI: Because you couldn't keep your mouth shut! That's why! Because of the things you said! Because of what you've done! You wanted to die and–

ERSILIA: And I should have died in silence, is that it? A hole in the ground and a stone over me and good riddance!

GROTTI: A stone and silence. Yes. Better that than what you did. But no, you had to make a racket, so you picked up your stone and threw it as hard as you could into the gutter at your feet. And the mud you raised has splashed on all of us, all over us!

ERSILIA: And how nicely it sticks to you!

GROTTI: While you go on sitting there, in the middle of your cesspool!

ERSILIA: You'd like to see me drown in it alone, wouldn't you? So you can all go back to what you were doing before: Franco, when he finds out about us, to his precious fiancée; you to your brilliant diplomatic career!

GROTTI: To my whole life, which you messed up so completely, damn you, burying me in your filth! What do you think, anyway? That the meaning of my entire life is to be found in those few hours we spent together? Look what they've cost me: the wreck of my whole life, the death of my child!

ERSILIA: That was your fault! Your fault! Do you think I'll ever forget the sight of that chair, there, against the railing of the terrace where I'd taken the baby? You didn't even give me time to take it away.

GROTTI: And what were you doing up there? You were supposed to stay close to my sick wife, near the room where she was sleeping—ready to go to her if she needed anything. What were you doing on the terrace?

ERSILIA: I had work to do. And the baby was playing.

GROTTI: No! You went there on purpose, so I'd come and look for you!

ERSILIA: Liar! You would have come for me wherever I was, even in the room next to your wife's!

GROTTI: No, no!

ERSILIA: Go ahead, deny it! As if you'd never done it before! And so, because I wasn't safe from you even there—

GROTTI: Because you wanted me! Because you wanted me!

ERSILIA: No! Because I couldn't resist your advances, your vile insinuations, and I'd always end up by wanting you—there, that's how you should put it! I was always so afraid your wife would hear us, so I—I— Oh, God, I know, I know now that something inside me warned me not to leave the chair there, that the baby playing on the terrace with her toys would be sure to climb up there and fall over the railing! I didn't heed the warning, I didn't listen, because you—do you remember?—you stood there in that doorway like an animal and you insisted, and insisted! And now I dream about it, I still dream about it—every night—I see it—there—the chair—and it's always the same—I see the baby—and I run to move it—and . . . and never in time . . . *(She begins to cry. A pause.)*

GROTTI *(absorbed, feeling a need to look at his life quite apart from the catastrophe that overwhelmed it, to explain himself to himself, as Ersilia continues to sob softly, convulsively)*: I worked hard . . . It was . . . it was as if I lived always outside of myself . . . Everything I did was for others . . . I thought only of my work . . . to fill the void I felt in my own life—the home I'd dreamed of and could never have, because the woman I married was always sick, moody, cold. . . . Then you came . . .

How did I treat you at first? How did I treat you?

ERSILIA *(tenderly, through her tears)*: You were very kind.

GROTTI: Because the more I suffered from the dreariness of my own life, the more I felt a need to be kind to others, to shift the whole weight of life onto my own shoulders so they at least could breathe a little more freely. Because of this need to bring happiness to others. That way, at least, I could share in it—I, who could never be happy myself. And when Laspiga stopped off there on his cruise, how did I depict you in his eyes? What didn't I tell him about you in order to be good to you, to make him fall in love with you? I even tried to be more affectionate than ever with my wife, so she'd be pleased and disposed to look favorably on your romance, the happy outcome of which I'd planned for your own good, planned only for the pleasure I would have derived from knowing I had been responsible for your happiness. And when I saw that you were in love with each other . . . No, no—it wasn't because I realized you'd gone too far, that you had gone to bed with him. That only angered my wife, not me—she lost all respect for you—

ERSILIA: But I'd never done that with anyone else before! Never! My head was in a whirl, spinning . . . It was the night before he left!

GROTTI: I know. I understood . . . I never thought of blaming you. And I never would have taken advantage of it if you—

ERSILIA: If I what?

GROTTI *(immediately)*: If you hadn't wanted me to! You . . . I don't know . . . the way you looked at me one evening as we left the table . . . Because you didn't believe! I felt you didn't believe I could be so kind to you only because I wanted to make you happy! Yes, that's it! And because you didn't believe it, you ruined everything. Because I needed your faith more than ever, to keep going, to overcome every temptation—

ERSILIA: But not from me! Not from me!

GROTTI: No! In myself! But if you had believed in my disinterest, if you had really trusted in my kindness, that animal lust would never have been aroused in me, suddenly like that, in all its desperate hunger. And even now, as I look at you—my baby dead—my whole life in ruins . . . *(He advances threateningly on her, with hatred in his eyes.)* No! Understand?

ERSILIA *(backing away, frightened)*: What do you want?

GROTTI: I want you to weep, to weep with me for the evil we've done!

ERSILIA: More than I have already?

GROTTI: I don't want to be the only one to suffer this way for the death of my baby! I won't let you go back to him, as if this horrible thing had never happened!

ERSILIA: No, no! I'd never do that! You know I wouldn't! Never! I'll stay here, with the man who took me in—

GROTTI: You can't! He doesn't want you! Can't you see he already agrees with Laspiga? They even left here together. By this time he's sick of you, and he thinks you're crazy not to accept the boy's offer and to send him away like that!

ERSILIA: But I told him I couldn't accept it.

GROTTI: Yes, but they both think you're just being obstinate and unreasonable! You haven't told him the real reason you can't accept!

ERSILIA: All right. If I have to, I will!

GROTTI: And then what you've done will seem so loathsome to him—the lies you told, the trouble you caused—a marriage broken off on the eve of the wedding, the scandal, the public sympathy you aroused so falsely, the pity you milked out of everyone—

ERSILIA *(crushed, hardly able to bear it)*: You're right . . . you're right . . . But I . . . I didn't want all this . . . I even told the old man I said what I did, lied like that, because I thought it was all over for me . . . These aren't things you can tell anyone! They're too ugly! Yes, too horrible . . . We can say them to each other, you and I —now, like this—because we share the same guilt . . . How can you want me, why do you want me to tell them the truth?

GROTTI: I was outraged at your lies. And when I heard from the girl's father what had happened—that the wedding was off and that Laspiga wanted to go back to you—I don't know how I managed to control myself in front of him. I rushed to the newspaper to deny everything you'd said about me. And you can't imagine how my wife felt when she found out! She wanted to go right to the girl and tell her everything—why you were thrown out, how she'd caught us together! I had to promise her, to assure her I'd at least prevent you from ruining anyone else's life. Do you understand?

ERSILIA: Yes, I understand. *(A pause. She stares darkly into space.)* All right. *(She rises. Another pause.)* Get out. I'll do it.

GROTTI *(looking at her, puzzled)*: What?

ERSILIA: You tell me I must—I'll do it.

GROTTI *(after a pause, continuing to stare at her)*: You're even more desperate than I am . . . Look at you . . . Look at what's happened to you . . . *(He goes to her and attempts to embrace her.)* Ersilia . . . Ersilia . . .

ERSILIA *(violently, proudly, fending him off)*: No, damn you, leave me alone!

GROTTI *(after her, reaching for her, wildly)*: No, no . . . listen, listen . . .

ERSILIA *(defending herself)*: Leave me alone, I said!

GROTTI *(continuing)*: Oh, God, let's cling together in our despair!

ERSILIA *(screaming)*: The baby! The baby!

GROTTI *(immediately letting her go and hiding his face in his hands)*: Murderess!
(A pause. He trembles violently.) God, I'm going mad . . . *(To her again:)* I need you, I need you . . . We're both so unhappy . . .

ERSILIA *(running to the windows)*: Get out . . . get out . . . I'll scream . . .

GROTTI *(following her)*: No . . . no . . . listen . . .

ERSILIA *(opening a window)*: I'll shout for help! There!
(The street noises gaily invade the room. Ersilia looks at Grotti, then gestures toward the door.)
Get out!

CURTAIN

ACT III

Ludovico Nota's apartment late afternoon of the same day. Mrs. Onoria stands at one of the open windows, apparently in the middle of a conversation with some other woman who must be leaning out of a window directly across the street. Emma is busy straightening up the room. The usual street noises are heard, but during the scene, as evening falls, they gradually die down.

ONORIA: Oh, yes, and then let me tell you what I— What's that? *(A pause.)* Until noon, but you know how it is—

it's not like getting a good night's sleep . . . *(A pause.)* What's that? I didn't hear you . . . *(A pause.)* Ah, yes. She left with Mr. Nota . . . Yes, for the suitcase. They wouldn't give it to him.

EMMA: And you'll see, they won't give it to her either.

ONORIA *(still talking out of the window)*: Well, they wouldn't go before.

EMMA: It won't be like this every day, I hope!

ONORIA *(turning to Emma)*: What are you grumbling about? I can't hear a thing!

EMMA: I mean, making up the rooms at this hour! It's almost dark out!

ONORIA *(to the window again)*: Mr. Nota must be one of those. Well, what can you expect from a man his age? *(She laughs.)* I think he wanted her to stay with him . . . *(A pause.)* Oh, no, she won't have anything to do with the other one . . . He must have been the one who kissed her . . . *(A pause, then in great excitement:)* No, no! Impossible! You must have seen wrong! Impossible! *(A pause, then she nods and waves her hand.)* Yes, all right. Good-by! Good-by! *(She closes the window.)* Can you imagine? She says she saw three men in here and that all three of them kissed her!

EMMA: Even that last one?

ONORIA: Impossible! It just couldn't have happened! Not all three of them!

EMMA: After you'd all gone, she and that consul were screaming at each other in here!

ONORIA: And didn't you . . . couldn't you hear what they said?

EMMA: Oh, I didn't go and put my ear to the door, if that's what you mean. I just happened to be passing by the foot of the stairs and heard them shouting, that's all. Her more than him, though.

ONORIA: I'd certainly like to know what else he wants from that poor creature. What was he doing here, after making all that trouble at the newspaper and saying he was going to sue everybody?

EMMA: Maybe he doesn't want her to get together with her fiancé.

ONORIA: And what business is that of his? Anyway, she doesn't want him back. Though I think she's wrong not to.

EMMA: She'd rather stay here with that old fool—

ONORIA: —who's already sick of her! Bored to death! I think he's already made that pretty clear to her.

EMMA: It might work out all right then. That way she can still change her mind and go back to that nice young man.

ONORIA: But maybe, you know, maybe she doesn't trust him any more. Though I really think he means it—he's really sorry now.

EMMA: Oh, I'm sure he is.

ONORIA: But she's worried about the other girl, the one he left to come back to her.

EMMA: I wouldn't be, I can tell you! She almost died because of him!

ONORIA: Well, she knows what it feels like to be abandoned, you see. It was so nice the way it was all written up in the paper. I think she hates him now. And she knows that here at least, with the old man . . . *(She makes a wry face.)* I saw her when she left with him. Her eyes were, I don't know, as if there was a veil over them. They were open, but she didn't see anything. She couldn't talk or even raise a finger. I asked her how she was, and she gave me such a strange smile I felt a chill all up my back. And her hand was like ice . . . *(She suddenly stops and listens. Then, in another voice:)* Oh, listen! That peddler again! Yes! Run down and get me that string I need! Just the small size, like I told you. I'll call him from up here.

(Emma runs out.)

(Onoria rushes to a window, opens it, leans out, shouting and signaling for the peddler to wait, then remains there.)

(Meanwhile, Franco appears in the doorway. He is very tense and upset.)

FRANCO *(raising his voice so as to be heard over the street noises)*: Excuse me! May I come in?

ONORIA *(turning and shutting the window)*: Oh, it's you, Mr. Laspiga? Come in, come in. She went out with Mr. Nota. They ought to be back any moment. *(Softly, insinuatingly.)* Keep after her, keep after her! You'll get her back!

(Before answering, Franco looks at her a moment as if he hadn't understood.)

FRANCO *(ironically, controlling his rage)*: Oh, yes! I'll keep after her, all right! You'll see!

ONORIA *(confidentially)*: That consul must have set her straight, you know! Oh, he set her straight, let me tell you!

FRANCO *(through clenched teeth)*: That bastard! That swine!

ONORIA: You're right! You're absolutely right! The poor child!

FRANCO *(exploding)*: Child? Don't make me laugh! You know what she is? A whore! A scheming little whore!

ONORIA *(shocked)*: Good God! What do you mean?

(Just then Ludovico enters from the street.)

LUDOVICO *(seeing Franco)*: Ah, back already? *(To Onoria:)* Hasn't she come in yet?

(Onoria turns to look at him, then, without answering, turns back to Franco.)

ONORIA: Are you serious?

LUDOVICO *(not understanding)*: What is it?

FRANCO *(resolutely, proudly, angrily)*: I'll tell you! This morning, when the noble Mr. Grotti's wife found out he'd come here to see his little slut–

LUDOVICO *(astounded)*: What?

ONORIA: Her? With the consul?

FRANCO: Yes, that's what I said! His little slut! Mrs. Grotti went to see my fiancée's family and revealed the whole affair!

LUDOVICO: Between Ersilia and her husband?

ONORIA: His mistress?

FRANCO: Exactly! But I still don't know whether it was before or after I asked her to marry me. That's what I came to find out! That's why I'm here now!

ONORIA: But how? But then . . . Oh, my God, I just can't believe it!

FRANCO: And do you know how, do you know when his wife found out about it? Just as the child was falling off the terrace!

ONORIA *(with a scream, covering her face)*: Oh!

FRANCO: She caught them together. And then she threw her out of the house. They'd gone off and left the baby alone.

ONORIA: They're murderers! Murderers! Both of them!

FRANCO: If he hadn't also been involved, she'd have gone to jail! And after having done all this, you understand–

ONORIA: Yes! She actually dared–

FRANCO: To come and cause all that trouble for me!

ONORIA: For all of us! We felt so sorry for her!

FRANCO: Do you realize what she's done to me?

LUDOVICO *(almost to himself)*: It seems incredible . . .

ONORIA: With that look of a holy martyr . . . Why, she's nothing but a fake!

FRANCO: Everything up in the air! A public scandal! My

fiancée disgraced! I nearly went out of my mind! Why I didn't I'll never know!

ONORIA: That's why, that's why she wanted to get away! The moment she saw you, the moment she heard Grotti was here! The fake! She knew her little game would be discovered! *(Angrily:)* Oh, but I'll get even with her for all the tears she's made me shed! *(To Ludovico:)* Out! Out with her! She's not going to stay here! I'm not going to have this kind of thing going on in my house! Oh, no! No, indeed!

LUDOVICO *(annoyed, shrugging her off)*: Now just wait a moment.

ONORIA: Wait? Oh, no, no, no! Out she goes! She can't stay here! Not in my house!

LUDOVICO: Oh, keep quiet, for God's sake! I still haven't got my bearings. *(To Franco:)* But why should the consul . . . ? *(He pauses.)* Don't you remember? It was Grotti, it was Grotti himself who was the first to protest against the story in the paper.

FRANCO: Of course!

LUDOVICO: What do you mean, of course? They'd stick together . . . I mean, if they were lovers . . .

FRANCO: But his wife is here with him! The woman she said all those terrible things about in the story!

LUDOVICO *(remembering)*: Ah, yes. That's right. Yes, I see. So that's why Ersilia was so upset when she found out what they'd said in the paper.

ONORIA: Claiming that the poor woman had sent her out of the house on some errand or other when the baby was killed!

FRANCO: It must have been the wife who forced him to go there and threaten to sue.

LUDOVICO: Then it's all a lie.

FRANCO: A vile, dirty lie!

LUDOVICO: Even that she tried to kill herself over you?

ONORIA: What I want to know is, how can anyone dare to lie so shamelessly!

LUDOVICO *(almost to himself, thoughtfully)*: Ah, yes . . . that's it . . . that's why she kept refusing to go back to you.

FRANCO: That would really have been the last straw!

ONORIA: Imagine! You poor man!

LUDOVICO *(more and more irritated by Onoria's clumsy remarks, which are also turning him against Franco)*: Now just a minute. You have to admit she did show some scruples at least once.

FRANCO: But when? Only when she saw me here ready to make amends for the wrong I thought I'd done.

LUDOVICO: I know, I know, but–

FRANCO: And even then, I want you to realize, her behavior yesterday is only acceptable under the best of circumstances. That is to say, if she became Grotti's mistress after I'd gone! If they were lovers before she met me, then I'm nothing but the victim–think of it!–the victim of the most humiliating swindle, all cooked up by the two of them!

LUDOVICO: No, that isn't–

FRANCO: As I told you, that's what I'm here to find out.

LUDOVICO: And what do you expect to do about it? I'm sorry, but you can't deny that she violently refused again and again to accept your offer.

FRANCO: I still want an answer from her! I want to know when!

LUDOVICO: I'm sorry, but, as far as you're concerned, I can't see how it matters. Whatever happened, you have no right to complain.

FRANCO: I don't? And why not? I–

LUDOVICO *(firmly)*: What she and Grotti did and when has

nothing to do with it! You were back here, about to marry somebody else!

FRANCO: Now just a minute—

LUDOVICO: Let me finish! You'd already paid her back, it seems to me, even before you found out what they'd done to you!

FRANCO: And my wrong excuses theirs? Is that what you mean?

LUDOVICO: Not at all. But it hardly gives you the right to demand an accounting from anyone. Be reasonable!

FRANCO *(forcefully)*: Oh, yes, it does! Yes, it does! Because they went all the way with their betrayal, they acted on it and completed it! While I, instead—I broke off my marriage and came running here!

LUDOVICO: Yes, when you found out she'd tried to kill herself—

FRANCO: But not over me! She admitted that herself! Well, I like that! Here you are, blaming me for what I've done, as if I were responsible for the whole sordid mess!

LUDOVICO: No, no. Look, I'm not blaming anyone. I simply wanted to show you that you're right in only one respect: that she did lie when she said—and had no right to say—that she'd killed herself because of you. But what I really can't understand is *why* she said such a thing. And when she was sure she was going to die, too. Certain kinds of lies can be useful if you want to live, but not if you expect to die. And it's very clear she herself realized how useless the lie was.

FRANCO: Useless? That's how you see it!

ONORIA: You simply won't stick to the facts!

LUDOVICO: Ah, the facts! I see! Very true! It's my most serious defect: I can never stick to the facts.

ONORIA: Well, at least you admit it. And you know what

the facts are? She didn't die—that's fact number one!

FRANCO: And the lie *was* useful to her! Oh, yes, very useful. If not because it brought me to her rescue—oh, that would have been the end!—at least because she found somebody like you.

ONORIA: Imagine! A writer!

LUDOVICO: Yes. An imbecile.

FRANCO *(quickly)*: I didn't say that.

LUDOVICO: Well, go ahead. Say it, say it!

ONORIA: Why don't you? If he admits it himself.

FRANCO: Oh, how flattered she must have been to see her imposture accepted, exalted in the realm of art—this romantic story of a suicide for love, no longer told by a mere journalist, but glorified by a writer of your reputation!

LUDOVICO: Yes. As a matter of fact, that's exactly what she wanted.

FRANCO: You see?

LUDOVICO: She was even disappointed I'd imagined it all happening to somebody else, somebody quite different.

ONORIA: Oh, they'd have made a lovely couple! Her spouting lies and him writing them all down!

LUDOVICO: Yes, lies. The lies we also call the art of fiction. Just because her story isn't true doesn't mean there's anything wrong with it, you know. In fact, if it's a really good story, then it matters quite a lot that it shouldn't be true. It may have worked out badly for her in real life, but this doesn't mean it won't succeed splendidly when I write it all down. And I'll tell you something else: this way it makes a much better story! Oh, much, much better! And I couldn't be happier that it's all come out! *(He indicates Onoria to Franco.)* Take her, for instance. First, she was all scorn and fury. Then all honey. And now nothing but bitterness and hatred—

ONORIA *(reacting angrily)*: And why shouldn't I be?

LUDOVICO *(quickly, approvingly)*: Oh, no reason at all! You're quite right! But it's a marvelous touch, you can't deny that! *(Turning to Franco:)* And look at you! Yesterday enraptured with your own nobility.

FRANCO *(also reacting angrily)*: You know why as well as I do!

LUDOVICO: Yes, yes, of course, and you were right! I admired you for it! And that's why it's so perfect now! What did you think, anyway? That I was going to stand around here and play the fool for you? No indeed! I'm simply going to amuse myself by showing you how lovely—how really lovely—how exquisite it all is, this comedy of a lie laid bare!

FRANCO *(wounded)*: Lovely, you said?

LUDOVICO *(understandingly)*: Yes, precisely because of what you've suffered and are suffering now. Oh, I understand, I know—believe me—I know what you're going through. And don't worry, I'll make it all seem terribly real, if I make a novel or a play out of it.

ONORIA: And you'd put me into it, too?

LUDOVICO: Only if I decide to turn it into a farce.

ONORIA: Ah, don't you dare! I warn you!

LUDOVICO: What would you do about it? Scream that it isn't true?

ONORIA: Yes! A lie! A lie! That you're a worse faker than she is!

LUDOVICO *(laughing)*: Don't worry! The critics wouldn't believe a word of it anyway! *(Suddenly serious again.)* Why isn't she back yet? She ought to be here by now . . . I gave her a little money . . .

ONORIA: Money? To her? Oh, brilliant! I can just imagine!

LUDOVICO: Only enough to pay her hotel bill and get her suitcase out.

ONORIA: If you gave her any money, she won't be back. You'll never see *her* again. So much for your plays and novels! At least I can rest easy on that score!

LUDOVICO: You're mistaken. I can always dream up a good ending, you know, even if in real life there isn't one.

FRANCO: Do you really think she won't come back?

LUDOVICO: Well, it depends. If the purpose of her lie can be explained by "sticking to the facts," as you put it, then I'm afraid she won't. She'll come back only if her purpose lies where I think it does—above and beyond mere facts. In which case I'll have my play. Though I'll have one even if she doesn't return.

FRANCO: Regardless of the facts?

LUDOVICO: The facts! The facts! My dear sir, the facts are what we assume them to be. In the life of the spirit there are no facts, but only life, as it appears to us in one form or another. The facts belong to the past, a past we've spiritually abandoned and therefore deprived of life. That's what you were saying here yesterday. And that's why I don't believe in facts.

(Emma enters.)

EMMA: The consul Grotti is here. He wants to see either Miss Drei or you, Mr. Nota.

LUDOVICO: Ah, so instead of her, we have him now!

FRANCO *(proudly and threateningly, starting for the door)*: And his timing is perfect!

LUDOVICO *(calmly and firmly, stepping in front of him)*: You will be kind enough not to cause any trouble in my house. And I tell you again that you have no right to demand anything from anyone!

FRANCO: I have a right to leave if I want to!

LUDOVICO: No! You'll stay here. I'll go and see him.

(Grotti appears in the doorway. He is very worried and excited.)

(Emma exits.)

GROTTI: Excuse me. Miss Drei?

ONORIA *(alarmed, annoyed)*: She's not here! She's gone!

FRANCO: And may never come back!

GROTTI: Do you know—Mr. Nota, can you tell me where—

LUDOVICO: You come bursting in here without my permission and I—

GROTTI: I'm terribly sorry! But I have to find out if Miss Drei knows that—that my wife—

FRANCO *(immediately)*:—went to my fiancée's family to denounce—

GROTTI *(quickly, shouting it)*:—her own madness!

FRANCO: So you deny it?

GROTTI *(furiously, scornfully)*: I neither admit nor deny anything! I have nothing to say to you!

FRANCO: You're wrong! You have to answer to me for—

GROTTI: For what? For the fact that my wife has gone mad? If you think there's anything to settle between us, come and see me about it in private whenever you wish!

FRANCO: I will!

GROTTI *(turning at once to Ludovico)*: All I need to find out, Mr. Nota, is whether Miss Drei knows about it!

LUDOVICO: I don't think she does.

GROTTI: Oh, thank God, thank God!

LUDOVICO: We left here together. I came back alone because she had to stop off at the hotel.

GROTTI: And you hadn't heard about it either?

LUDOVICO: No. When I returned, I found Mr. Laspiga here and he told me.

GROTTI: Good, good! Because in her present state of desperation this new blow . . .

LUDOVICO: The fact is, we've been waiting for her—and she hasn't come back yet.

FRANCO: Even if she doesn't know about it, she probably expected it to happen. And since Mr. Nota gave her some money, she may have run off somewhere.

GROTTI: My God, I hope so! But I'm afraid she's probably—

FRANCO: So you do admit it!

GROTTI: I admit nothing!

FRANCO: Your sense of chivalry, no doubt!

GROTTI: Can't you understand, Laspiga, that I don't give a damn what you believe or don't believe? You can believe anything you like, anything you please!

FRANCO *(angrily, proudly)*: I can? Just anything I please? I want to know the truth!

GROTTI: And what then? Suppose I told you my wife was lying? Would you believe me? In any case, what happened to this girl is your fault, yours and no one else's!

FRANCO: My fault? Only mine?

GROTTI: Yes!

FRANCO: But if she was innocent when your wife threw her out, innocent even of the death of the child—

GROTTI *(immediately, firmly)*: Of that, no!

FRANCO: So she did lie about that?

GROTTI: Yes. I went to the newspaper office to protest that very lie.

FRANCO: And then you came here to get your story straight with her? Is that it?

GROTTI *(trembling, barely able to restrain himself, apologizing to Ludovico)*: You must excuse me, sir. *(To Franco again:)* I came here because your prospective father-in-law begged me to and I found her in despair—we all saw how she was—because you—

FRANCO *(quickly, forcefully)*:—because I wanted to atone for all the wrong I'd done her! Why in despair, I'd like to know, if I was really to blame for everything?

GROTTI: Because she didn't want to go back to you, that's why! Oh, you're incredible! She doesn't want you! She doesn't want you! She told you so! Over and over! My God, can't you get that through your head?

FRANCO: It doesn't make my situation any easier! Anything but! You'd like to see me step out of the picture, wouldn't you, so you could easily play your part for his benefit *(indicating Ludovico)* and convince him none of it is true! But I'm here, not because I want to be, but because she herself publicly declared that she had killed herself for my sake!

GROTTI: And hasn't she already told you she was lying?

FRANCO *(quickly, violently)*: So another lie! That makes two! And I suppose you think I forced her to tell all those lies?

GROTTI: Perhaps you did, who knows? Perhaps that's why she said no to you.

FRANCO: So then it might be true that I was the reason behind her suicide attempt?

GROTTI: I don't know. I only know she did it.

FRANCO: If it's the way you say it is, then she did it over me, because I was about to marry someone else. I can't see any other reason why she'd do it, can you?

LUDOVICO: Unless it was because of what she told me—

FRANCO *(turning quickly on him)*: No, I'm sorry, but you said earlier you couldn't see any other reason for it!

LUDOVICO: Well, you see, she had nothing left . . . out there, in the street . . . like a beggar . . .

FRANCO *(ironically)*: Ah, yes! That night when she offered herself to the first man who came along . . .

GROTTI *(darkening)*: She said that?

FRANCO *(loudly, heatedly)*: Yes! Yes, she did! And only because of what I'd done to her, because I'd betrayed her! And knowing all this, you'd still expect me not to go on insisting with every ounce of my strength, with all my heart and soul, that she accept my offer? I'd still insist, even now, if you give me your word of honor that your wife was lying when she said you two had been lovers!

(At this point Emma runs in, screaming in terror.)

EMMA: Help! Oh, my God, come quickly! Please . . . !

ONORIA: What is it?

LUDOVICO: Ersilia?

EMMA: Yes, sir . . . she's back . . .

GROTTI: Where is she?

ONORIA: Where?

EMMA: Like a corpse . . . I just opened the door . . . she—she fell inside . . . holding her suitcase . . .

LUDOVICO: The poison—she kept the poison in her suitcase . . .

(As they all start to rush for the door, Ersilia suddenly appears on the threshold. She is deathly pale, but very calm. Her expression is soft, almost smiling. They all freeze at the sight of her, as if afraid to move.)

ONORIA: Oh . . . it's her . . .

GROTTI *(in a sudden outburst)*: Ersilia . . . Ersilia . . . what have you done?

FRANCO *(softly, almost to himself)*: So, it is true!

LUDOVICO *(starting to move to her aid)*: Ersilia . . .

ONORIA *(annoyed, to herself)*: Oh, not again.

ERSILIA: It's nothing. Hush . . . Nothing at all, this time . . . *(She makes a gesture for silence, raising her index finger to her lips.)*

GROTTI *(with a cry)*: No! No! My God, my God, we've got to help her! Quickly! Let's get her out of here!

ONORIA *(frightened)*: Yes, yes! Right away, at once!

LUDOVICO *(going to Ersilia)*: Yes . . . come . . .

ERSILIA *(drawing away from him)*: No! I won't! I don't want to! Please!

GROTTI *(also running to her)*: You must! Come, come with me! I'll take you!

ERSILIA: I said I don't want to.

LUDOVICO: But you must! Please! You need a doctor! Ersilia!

ONORIA: I'll send for a cab!

ERSILIA: Please! Stop it! I don't want to. It's too late.

GROTTI: How do you know? We mustn't lose any time!

ERSILIA: I tell you it's too late. It's all over. Just keep quiet, please. A little peace. Mr. Nota, if you'd be so kind . . . *(To Onoria:)* And you . . . It will take a little time . . . I'm sorry . . . But not long, I hope . . .

LUDOVICO: What is it? Tell me. What do you want?

ERSILIA: Your bed.

LUDOVICO: Of course. This way.

ONORIA: This way, this way.

GROTTI *(in another violent outburst)*: What have you done? What have you done?

LUDOVICO: You could have stayed here. You could always have stayed with me.

ERSILIA: No. If I hadn't done it, no one would ever have believed me.

FRANCO *(deeply moved)*: What? What did you want us to believe?

ERSILIA *(peacefully)*: That I didn't lie because I wanted to live. That's all.

FRANCO: Why then?

ERSILIA: So I could die. There. You see? I shouted it at you, that I thought it was all over and that I lied only because I thought I was dying. You didn't want to believe me. And you were right not to. Yes, you were right. I never thought I'd upset you, I'd hurt you like this. I despised myself so much!

FRANCO: What do you mean? You accused me–

ERSILIA: No.

FRANCO: But–

ERSILIA: No, I didn't . . . It's so hard to explain it . . . let alone make you believe it . . . But now I'll try . . . I despised myself so much that I never dreamed I could cause you such a lot of trouble. . . . You can believe that. You see–I wanted first of all to establish my right to be believed–this way–so I could say this to you . . . I caused you all this trouble, and your fiancée, too, and I knew, I knew I shouldn't have done it–that I had no right to do it because . . . because . . . *(She looks at Grotti, then turns back to Franco:)* You found out about it? From his wife, didn't you?

FRANCO *(almost inaudibly)*: Yes.

ERSILIA: I knew you would. And he came here to deny it, didn't he?

FRANCO: Yes.

ERSILIA: There. You see? *(She looks at him and makes a gesture of sorrowful pity, a slight opening of her hands —a gesture that wordlessly but eloquently explains why martyred humanity feels the need to lie. Then, very softly, she says:)* And you, too . . .

FRANCO *(moved, with an impulse of sincerity, understanding her gesture)*: Yes . . . Yes, I also lied!

ERSILIA *(smiling abstractedly)*: You told me your dream once . . . You said . . . I don't know . . . so many beautiful things to me . . . And then you came here to make amends . . . Yes, just as he—to make amends—denied everything.

(Grotti begins to sob violently. Disturbed, Ersilia signs to him to control himself and be still.)

No, no, please! It's only that we all, we all want to make a good impression. The more . . . the more hor— *(She wants to say "horrible," but she is so overcome with disgust and pity that she can barely get it out.)* —the more horrible we are, the more beautiful we want to seem, that's all. *(She smiles again.)* Oh, God, yes—to hide our nakedness in decent clothing, that's all. I had nothing to wear to come and see you in when I got back. And then I heard that you, too . . . yes, that you'd taken off that lovely sailor's uniform. And then you saw me that night . . . you saw me there, in the street, with nothing left . . . and . . . and . . . *(Her face clouds over at the memory of that night.)* Yes, just one more handful of mud on me—to leave me soaking in my own filth . . .

Oh, God, how awful! How disgusting! And then . . . and then I only wanted to make myself a decent little dress to die in. There, you see why I lied? That's the only reason, I swear it! My whole life I'd never been able to wear one, to make some sort of impression on anyone. It was always torn away from me by all the dogs—the dogs who waited for me everywhere, in every street—no dress that wasn't immediately soiled by all the filth of the streets—and so I wanted one nice one—one beautiful one—to die in—the most beautiful of all—the one I'd dreamed of back there—a bridal gown—but only to die in, to die in, that's all—you see—a few tears shed over me, nothing more. Well, I couldn't have it! Not even to die in! Torn off my back, stripped off my body! No! I had to die naked! Exposed, disgraced, scorned! So here I am at last. Are you all satisfied? And now leave me alone. . . . Go away and let me die in silence—naked. Please go. I have a right to say it now, don't I? That I don't want to see anyone. Or talk to anyone. Go, go and tell your wife—tell your fiancée—that this corpse—yes—this corpse died naked. . . .

CURTAIN

THE RULES OF THE GAME

(Il giuoco delle parti)

CHARACTERS

LEONE GALA
SILIA GALA
GUIDO VENANZI
DR. SPIGA
BARELLI
FILIPPO
MARQUIS MIGLIORITI
CLARA
FIRST DRUNK
SECOND DRUNK
THIRD DRUNK
THE NEIGHBORS (Three Men and Two Women)

ACT I

The living room of Silia's home, in any large Italian city. Evening.

ACT II

Leone's combination dining room and studio. Late the following morning.

ACT III

Leone's house. Early the following morning.

TIME: *The present.*

ACT I

Silia Gala's luxuriously furnished living room. Evening.

The French doors leading into the dining room are open. Guido Venanzi, in evening clothes, is standing by the dining-room table over a large silver tray crowded with bottles. Silia, dressed in a provocatively low-cut negligee, is in the living room, slumped in an easy chair. She is absorbed in her own thoughts.

GUIDO: Chartreuse? *(He waits for her reply, then, when she doesn't answer, continues:)* Anisette? Cognac? Well, then, I'll do the honors myself. *(He pours an anisette, walks over to Silia, and offers it to her.)* Here.

SILIA *(ignoring him at first, then suddenly reacting with irritation to his presence)*: Oooff!

GUIDO *(he drains the glass and bows ironically to her)*: And thanks for the trouble. I really didn't want it for myself. *(He returns the glass to the dining room, comes back, sits down, and looks at Silia, who has resumed her former attitude.)* If you'd only tell me what's the matter with you!

SILIA: Where do you think I am right now? Here?

GUIDO: Well, where are you? Somewhere outside?

SILIA *(very annoyed)*: Yes, outside! Outside! Anywhere but here!

GUIDO *(softly to himself)*: So I'm alone. All right. Then I'll see what I can steal. *(He rises, pretends to look around, approaches Silia as if unaware of her presence, then stops and looks at her with astonishment.)* Oh, look! What's this? Your body, left here, in this chair? Ah, I'll take it at once! *(He starts to embrace her, but she leaps to her feet and pushes him away.)*

SILIA: Stop it! I said no! No, no, and no!

GUIDO: Back already? Too bad! I guess your husband was right when he said that what we seek on the outside is really within ourselves.

SILIA: That's the fourth or fifth time you've mentioned my husband this evening.

GUIDO: It seems to be the only way I can get you to talk to me.

SILIA: No, darling, it just makes you even more insufferable.

GUIDO: Thank you.

SILIA *(after a long pause, then completely absorbed in her vision)*: I could see it so clearly!

GUIDO: What?

SILIA: Perhaps I've said it already . . . But it was so clear . . . all of it . . . that soft, faraway smile . . .

GUIDO *(completely confused)*: Who?

SILIA: While she . . . I don't know . . . I couldn't see her hands . . . but that must be the way the women do it there, while the men are out fishing. Yes . . . those little islands . . . near Iceland . . .

GUIDO: You were dreaming about Iceland?

SILIA: Yes . . . this way . . . this way! *(She waves her fingers, acting out her fantasy. A pause, then exploding again.)* It has to end! It simply has to end! Don't you understand that it can't go on like this?

GUIDO: Are you talking to me?

SILIA: I was talking to myself.

GUIDO: Yes, but it was all for my benefit, wasn't it?

SILIA *(annoyed)*: Oh, God! You see everything in miniature. Even yourself. There you are—you, at the center of a circumscribed, precisely defined little universe! To you, I suppose, the word geography means only that funny colored book you were made to study as a child.

GUIDO *(confused)*: Geography?

SILIA: Remember? With all those place names your teacher made you learn by heart?

GUIDO: Ah, yes! What a bore that was!

SILIA: But the rivers, the mountains, the countries, the islands, the continents—they *do* really exist. Did you know that?

GUIDO: What? Oh, thanks for telling me.

SILIA: And while we sit here, in this room, those places exist—people actually *live* there.

GUIDO *(the light dawning)*: Ah, that's it! You need a change. Darling, why don't we take a trip?

SILIA: There you are again! You and I on a nice little trip. Can't you see anything outside of yourself? Can't you imagine something—something grand? A life entirely different? This one has become so unbearable, I'm suffocating!

GUIDO: But what kind of a life do you want, Silia?

SILIA: I don't know. Any kind! Anything but this! Oh, God, for a breath, just for a breath of hope, something that would let in a little air! I tell you that would be enough! I could live on that breath of air alone, without even running to the window to see what's out there, waiting for me!

GUIDO: You sound as if you were in prison!

SILIA: I am in prison!

GUIDO: And who keeps you there?

SILIA: You . . . everyone . . . myself . . . this body of mine. When I forget I'm a woman— Ah, no, I'm never allowed to forget that, not from the way you all look at me . . . at my woman's body. Sometimes, though, I actually do forget I am a woman . . . who thinks about that? . . . and I look around. And all of a sudden I see those great big eyes . . . Oh, God, I have to burst out laughing every time! And so I say to myself, "Well, well, you're really a woman, a woman . . ."

GUIDO: It seems to me you don't have much to complain about.

SILIA: No, I suppose not, because . . . because I'm pleasing . . . But no one ever thinks about me, when I don't feel like being a woman.

GUIDO *(meaningfully)*: Tonight, for instance.

SILIA: I've never enjoyed being a woman. Never.

GUIDO: Not even when you could make a man suffer?

SILIA: Ah, yes, I've often enjoyed that part of it.

GUIDO: Tonight, for instance.

SILIA *(after a pause, then bursting out again with renewed anguish)*: But your real life—the one you admit to no one else, not even to yourself!

GUIDO: What are you talking about?

SILIA: Didn't you ever discover yourself suddenly in a mirror, catch yourself unaware so that your own image seems strange to you, disconcerts you, upsets your whole concept of yourself? It's a moment that passes as quickly as it comes—some familiar little gesture recalls you to yourself . . . I don't know . . . a hand raised to push away a stray curl . . .

GUIDO: Yes? Well?

SILIA: Don't you understand? The mirror usually reflects only the way others see us, the way we are expected to behave, forced to behave—hardly ever what we really are . . . Oh, I can't stand it any more!

GUIDO *(quietly)*: Shall I tell you why you're raving like this?

SILIA *(turning on him)*: Because I have to look at you!

GUIDO: Thanks. Then you want me to go?

SILIA: Yes, go! Go!

GUIDO *(pleading)*: But why, Silia?

SILIA: Because I don't want you to–

GUIDO *(interrupting)*: No, I– Why do you treat me so badly?

SILIA: I don't treat you badly. I just don't want you to be seen here too often, that's all.

GUIDO: Too often? I hardly ever come here! It's been over a week since the last time, you know that! Time passes pretty quickly for you.

SILIA: Quickly? Every moment is an eternity!

GUIDO: So then I don't exist in your life.

SILIA: Oh, God, Guido, please . . .

GUIDO: Every day I waited for you. You never let me see you.

SILIA: What do you expect to see? Look at me!

GUIDO: The trouble is, you don't know what you want . . . and so, without knowing what you want, you beg for some vague breath of hope, a little opening on the future . . .

SILIA: Yes, because the way you see it, I ought to approach the future with a measuring tape in my hands. I ought to want exactly so much and not an inch more. As if life were a nice little house to be furnished with just the right little pieces.

GUIDO: If you enjoy thinking of me as a pedant–

SILIA: Yes, my dear. Every time you open your mouth it's a yawn!

GUIDO: Thank you.

SILIA: You'd like me to understand that I've always had everything I've wanted, and that now I'm raving on like this–that's how you put it–because I want the impossible, isn't that so? It's not sensible. Well, I know it. But what can be done about it? The impossible is what I want!

GUIDO: For example?

SILIA: For example? Well, what have I ever had? Can you tell me what I've ever had to be happy about?

GUIDO: I don't even mean happiness, if nothing can make you happy . . .

SILIA: Then what *are* you talking about?

GUIDO: Happiness is a question of proportion. I mean, one person is happy with so much— *(he measures it between thumb and forefinger)*—another has everything and isn't happy.

SILIA: I have everything?

GUIDO: No . . . I meant . . .

SILIA: Explain yourself.

GUIDO: No, you explain! What more could you want?

SILIA *(imitating him)*: I am rich . . . independent . . . free . . . *(Changing tone, heatedly:)* But can't you understand that this is his way of revenging himself?

GUIDO: That's your fault! Because you don't know how to enjoy the freedom he gave you—

SILIA: —the freedom to have you or anybody else make love to me . . . to stay here or go somewhere else . . . to be free, entirely free . . . But I am not free.

GUIDO: You're not?

SILIA: I mean free to do as I like, as if there were no one else!

GUIDO: But who's stopping you?

SILIA: He is! I can't get him out of my mind! The expression on his face when he gave me my freedom, as if it were nothing at all, going off by himself like that. And I'm not free, I know it. For three years we've lived like this, and no matter what I do, I'm still his slave. See that? That's his chair. Look at it! It sits there as if it still belonged to him, as if it were a part of him and had nothing to do with me!

GUIDO: But this is an obsession of yours.

SILIA: The man haunts me!

GUIDO: You never see him.

SILIA: But he's here! He's here! And I'll never get rid of him as long as I know he exists! Oh, God, if he'd only die!

GUIDO: Silia, excuse me, but doesn't he still stop by every evening for half an hour?

SILIA: Not even that. And it was agreed that he would come, come to see me every evening for half an hour! Every evening!

GUIDO: And, in fact, he does come, doesn't he? He remains downstairs and sends the maid up to ask if there's anything new.

SILIA: That's not enough. He must come up! He must! And he must stay here half an hour every evening, as agreed.

GUIDO: Excuse me, but you said—

SILIA: What did I say? Did I contradict myself?

GUIDO: You said the man haunts you.

SILIA: No. I meant that he exists, that he's alive—that's what haunts me! It's not his physical presence . . . In fact, when he comes up, it's better, because I can see him . . . He comes in, he sits there . . . like anybody else, no better and no worse than anybody else . . . and I look into his eyes . . . Those hateful eyes! God! Horrible eyes! Blank and at the same time as sharp as needles . . . And the sound of his voice grates on my nerves . . . But at least I can rejoice in the bother I've caused him by making him come upstairs, all for nothing!

GUIDO: I don't believe it.

SILIA: What don't you believe?

GUIDO: That anything could bother him.

SILIA: Ah, then you know? That's just it! After he goes, I sit here for hours on end, crushed by the idea that such a man can exist, that anyone can be so removed from life and yet weigh so heavily on the lives of others.

He looks down on everybody—like a famous chef over his delicacies, ladies and gentlemen—looks down and understands everything, every little thing, every movement, every gesture. He anticipates everything you are about to do and so deprives you of the pleasure of doing it. The man has paralyzed me! I'm continually obsessed with one idea—how to get rid of him, to destroy him! Not only for my sake, but for everybody's!

GUIDO: Oh, come, come, Silia.

SILIA: It's true! I swear it!

(There is a knock at the door.)

CLARA: Excuse me . . .

SILIA: Yes, Clara?

CLARA *(appearing in the entrance)*: Mr. Gala is downstairs.

SILIA: Ah, he's here!

CLARA: He wants to know if there's anything new.

SILIA: Yes. Tell him to come up! Tell him to come up!

CLARA: At once, madam.

(Clara exits.)

GUIDO: But why tonight, Silia? The one evening I'm here?

SILIA: That's the best possible reason.

GUIDO: No . . . please . . .

SILIA: Yes! To punish you for having come at all! And now I'll leave him to you. I'm going to bed. *(She starts out.)*

GUIDO *(running to stop her)*: No, for God's sake! Are you crazy? What will he say?

SILIA: What do you expect him to say?

GUIDO: No . . . listen . . . it's late . . .

SILIA: So much the better.

GUIDO: No, no, Silia! You're just trying to test him. It's madness!

SILIA *(wrenching free of him)*: I don't want to see him!

GUIDO: Neither do I, for God's sake!

SILIA: You talk to him!

GUIDO: Oh, no, thank you! He's not going to find me here!

(Silia exits to her room as Guido runs into the dining room, closing the French doors behind him.)

LEONE *(off stage)*: May I come in? *(He opens the door and sticks his head in.)* Excuse me, may I— *(He sees the room is empty.)* Ah . . . *(He looks around.)* Well, well. *(He immediately erases the expression of surprise from his features, takes his watch out of his pocket, looks at it, then walks over to the fireplace and adjusts the hands of the clock on the mantelpiece, which promptly strikes twice. He puts his watch back into his pocket and sits down, calmly and impassively prepared to wait out the time agreed upon. After a brief pause, there is the sound of a whispered argument from behind the French doors: Silia is forcing Guido to come out of hiding. Leone does not even turn to look in that direction and, after a moment or two, one of the doors opens and Guido appears.)*

GUIDO: Oh, Leone . . . I just dropped in for a little glass of chartreuse.

LEONE: At ten-thirty?

GUIDO: Yes . . . As a matter of fact, I was on my way out when—

LEONE: That isn't what I meant. What kind of chartreuse, green or yellow?

GUIDO: I . . . I don't remember . . . Green, I think.

LEONE: At about two o'clock you'll dream you are chewing on a dead lizard.

GUIDO *(grimacing)*: Chewing on a what?

LEONE: A lizard. It's the one sure effect of drinking liqueurs too late after dinner . . . And Silia?

GUIDO *(embarrassed)*: Oh . . . She was in there, with me.

LEONE: And where is she now?

GUIDO: I don't know. She . . . she made me come in when she heard you were here. Maybe she'll join us.

LEONE: Is there anything new?

GUIDO: Not as far as I know.

LEONE: Then why did she make me come upstairs?

GUIDO: I was about to leave when the maid said that you . . . I don't know . . . that you were downstairs.

LEONE: I stop by every evening.

GUIDO: Yes, but . . . I guess she wanted you to come up.

LEONE: Did she say so?

GUIDO: Yes. Yes, she did.

LEONE: She's angry?

GUIDO: A little. I guess it's because . . . I don't know . . . It must be something about the agreement you made when you so tastefully—

LEONE: Taste had nothing to do with it.

GUIDO: I mean, without scandal . . .

LEONE: Scandal? Why should there be a scandal?

GUIDO: Well, without going to court—

LEONE: A waste of time.

GUIDO: When you separated without quarreling, that's what I mean.

LEONE: Why should I quarrel with anyone? I've always said yes to everybody.

GUIDO: That's true. In fact, it's an enviable quality of yours. But perhaps—you'll excuse me for saying it—perhaps you go a little too far.

LEONE: You think so?

GUIDO: Yes, because, you see, sometimes you— *(He looks at Leone and stops.)*

LEONE: I what?

GUIDO: You upset people.

LEONE: That's a good one! I upset people? Who, for instance?

GUIDO: You upset them because . . . well, by doing everything others do . . . by doing everything others want you to do . . . I'll bet that if your wife said to you, "Let's fight!" . . .

LEONE: I'd answer, "Let's fight!"

GUIDO: So when she said, "Let's separate!" . . .

LEONE: I said, "All right, let's separate!"

GUIDO: You see? Then if your wife had shouted, "But this way we can't fight!"

LEONE: I would have told her, "Then, my dear, let's not fight!"

GUIDO: But don't you realize this is what upsets everybody? You behave as if you weren't there. I mean, it's all right up to a point, but after a while people begin to feel themselves blocked, helpless. Because—because, after all, you do exist.

LEONE: That's right—I exist. *(Another pause, then sharply:)* Shouldn't I?

GUIDO: My God, of course! I didn't say you shouldn't!

LEONE: But, my dear Guido, I would prefer not to. However, I do my best to exist as little as possible, for others as well as myself. The facts are to blame, my friend. We are all imprisoned by facts: I was born, I exist. Facts. People ought to be a little more considerate of my inability to disappear entirely. You see, I married her. Or, to be more accurate, I allowed her to marry me. Another fact, another prison! What can you do? She immediately began to twist and turn, to rant, to rage, anything to escape . . . and I . . . I assure you, Guido, I suffered a great deal . . . Then we hit on this solution. I left her everything, taking only my books and my kitchen utensils—the things I absolutely can't do without. But I know it's useless. The part assigned to me by another indestructible fact remains: I am the husband. Everybody also ought to bear that in mind. Oh, well! You know how the blind are, my friend?

GUIDO: The blind?

LEONE: They can never stand next to anything. Tell a blind man groping for something that he's standing next to it, he'll immediately turn and bump into it. And that's how it is with her—never beside you, always against. *(A pause. He looks toward the French doors.)* I guess she doesn't want to come in. *(He takes his watch out, sees that his half-hour is not yet up, and replaces it.)* You don't know if there was anything she wanted to tell me?

GUIDO: No, I don't think there was anything.

LEONE: Then this whim for— *(He makes a gesture indicating "the two of us.")*

GUIDO *(not understanding)*: For what?

LEONE: This business of throwing the two of us together, face to face.

GUIDO: Maybe she thinks that I've—

LEONE:—already gone? *(He shakes his finger.)* She'd come in.

GUIDO *(starting to go)*: Oh, then I'll—

LEONE *(immediately stopping him)*: No, please. I'll be gone in a moment. If there wasn't anything she wanted to tell me . . . *(A pause, then he gets up.)* Ah, it's a sad thing, my friend, to have understood the game.

GUIDO: What game?

LEONE: Any game. This one, for instance. The game of life.

GUIDO: You understand it?

LEONE: For some time now. And also the way to win it.

GUIDO: I wish I knew the answer!

LEONE: Ah, Guido, there's no way out for you. To win the game you have to know how to defend yourself. But a certain kind of defense— Let's call it a desperate one, something you probably couldn't understand.

GUIDO: What do you mean by desperate? Ferocious?

LEONE: No, no. Desperate in the most profound sense, an emotion stripped of even the lingering trace of bitterness.

GUIDO: But what sort of defense?

LEONE: The strongest, the most unshakable. You must give up all hope, because only the absence of hope makes it impossible for you to compromise.

GUIDO: I don't understand. You call that a defense? What are you defending, if that's how you feel about things? *(Leone glances at him darkly, then reassumes his serene expression.)*

LEONE: Nothing, if you succeed, as I did, in draining yourself of every emotion. You must defend yourself from others and above all from yourself, from the pain which life inevitably inflicts on everyone, the pain I suffered for her . . . *(indicating the French doors behind which Silia is hiding)* . . . the pain I cause her even now, the pain you cause me–

GUIDO: I?

LEONE: Of course. Inevitably. *(Peering into his eyes.)* Do you think you don't?

GUIDO: Well . . . not as far as I know . . .

LEONE: Oh, even without knowing it, my friend. You eat meat, don't you? Who provides it for you? A chicken or a calf–a living, breathing animal. No, we make each other suffer all the time and nothing can be done about it. That's the way life is. You have to drain yourself of it.

GUIDO: Fine! And what's left?

LEONE: The pleasure, not of living for yourself, but of seeing how others live; not of acting for yourself, but of watching yourself in action–for those few years you're forced to exist.

GUIDO: I'm sorry, but that's not enough.

LEONE: True, but there is one marvelous compensation: the play of the intellect that clarifies the chaos of your passions, that outlines clearly and precisely all that moves within you so tumultuously. You understand, however, that it would be very dangerous to enjoy this lucid and tranquil emptiness you make within yourself because, among other things, you run the risk of soaring too high among the clouds, like a balloon, unless you place within yourself, with artistry and perfect skill, the exact counterweight.

GUIDO: Ah! That's why you like to eat so much!

LEONE: That's the way I keep my balance. You have to remain always on your feet, like those strange toys which, no matter how you push them, always bounce back upright. That's all we are, believe me. But you have to know how to do it, how to empty yourself and find your counterweight. Otherwise, you risk being caught in some particularly ludicrous position. In other words, my friend, the secret of living is to find a pivot, the pivot of a concept on which you can make your stand.

GUIDO: Oh, no, no! Thanks a lot, but that's not for me. And it's not so easy.

LEONE: True. You can't buy concepts in wholesale lots. You have to work them out yourself, one to suit every occasion. And they have to be good ones or when fate takes you violently unawares, they'll blow up in your face.

GUIDO: Oh, but the things that can happen to you in life, Leone!

LEONE: I know. That's why I like to cook and eat well. A good meal is a great concept. And, after all, fate never— But you mustn't worry too much about what life can do to you, Guido. After all, what can happen?

GUIDO: All sorts of things. Terrible things.

LEONE: Yes, but it depends how you cope with them. That's what I was telling you. You have to be alert and keep your emotions under control. Then you can immediately seize the event, understand it, and play with it. Look, it's as if someone suddenly threw an egg at you.

GUIDO: An egg?

LEONE: Yes.

GUIDO: How about a bullet?

LEONE: Then the game is over. There's no sense even talking about it.

GUIDO: But why an egg?

LEONE: Just another way of putting it. If you aren't ready for it, it will either hit you or you'll drop it. In either case, it will probably splatter all over you. But if you're ready for it, you catch it, punch a hole in each end, and suck it out. Then what are you left with?

GUIDO: An empty shell.

LEONE: That's it! That's the concept! You can play with the shell, bounce it from one hand to another, throw it up into the air and catch it, then—wham!—you crush it in your hands and throw it away!

(There is a burst of laughter from behind the half-open door where Silia is hiding.)

SILIA *(from the dining room)*: I'm not an empty shell in your hands!

(Leone whirls and goes right up to the French doors.)

LEONE: Oh, no, Silia! The next time you throw yourself at me, I'll catch you, punch a hole in each end, and suck you up! *(No sooner has he spoken than Silia, without showing herself, slams the open half of the door in his face. Leone stands there a moment, shaking his head, then turns back to Guido.)* It's a great loss to me, Guido. Living with her was an extraordinary experience. I miss it. *(Indicating Silia in the next room.)* She was always unhappy, because she was so full of life. Not just one life, but many of them. But no matter what she tried, she never learned to keep her balance. She can never be happy, either alone or with anyone else.

(Guido, absorbed in his own problem, shakes his head sadly.)

You agree?

GUIDO *(starting)*: What? Oh, yes. Yes, you're absolutely right.

LEONE: But you have no idea what riches are within her. She has certain qualities you'd never even suspect, not because they don't exist, but because you ignore them, because you only see her the way she seems to you. Would you believe, for example, that sometimes she sings to herself? Yes, it's true. Some mornings I'd hear her voice going from room to room—a nice, shaky little voice, almost like a child's. She's another person then, someone else entirely, and she doesn't even realize it. When she forgets herself like that, she's a child, a baby. And then sometimes she'll be dreaming about something, her eyes focused on some bright distant place, her fingers toying absently with the little curls on the back of her neck. Can you tell me who she is then? Someone else, someone she doesn't know, someone who can never exist. Say to her, "That's the way I want you, that's the way you ought to be." She'll ask you, "How is that?" "The way you were just now." "How was I?" "You were singing." "I was singing?" "Yes, and playing with your hair, like this . . ." She doesn't know; she'd deny it. She wouldn't recognize herself at all in what you saw because you can only see her through your own eyes, not hers. It's really too bad, my friend. This sweet and lovely potential within her, wasted.
(There is a long, sad pause, then the clock on the mantelpiece strikes the hour.)
Ah, eleven o'clock. Say good-by to her for me. *(He hurries toward the exit.)*

SILIA *(quickly opening the French doors)*: No, wait! Wait a moment!

LEONE: Oh, no! My half-hour is up.

SILIA: I wanted to give you this! *(Laughing, she tosses him an empty eggshell.)*

LEONE: Ah, but I didn't suck this one. Here . . . *(walking quickly over to Guido)* . . . let's give it to him!

(Guido automatically takes the shell and stands there as Leone exits laughing.)

SILIA: Why doesn't someone kill him?!

GUIDO: By God, I'm going to bounce this off his head! *(He runs toward the window.)*

SILIA *(laughing)*: Yes, yes! Give it to me! I'll do it! I'll do it! *(she snatches the shell from Guido.)*

GUIDO: Do you think you can?

SILIA: Yes. From here. *(She leans out the window to look, alert and ready to throw down the eggshell.)* As he steps out of the door . . .

GUIDO *(behind her)*: Careful . . . careful now . . .

(Silia throws the eggshell and immediately steps back with a cry.)

SILIA: Oh, God!

GUIDO: What happened?

SILIA: My God!

GUIDO: You hit someone else?

SILIA: Yes. A gust of air caught it.

GUIDO: Of course. It was too light. You should have let me do it.

SILIA: They're coming up!

GUIDO: Who?

SILIA: There was a group of four men . . . standing near the door . . . As he went out, they came in . . . Perhaps they live here.

GUIDO: Well, what does it matter? *(Taking advantage of her dismay, he takes her in his arms.)*

SILIA: I think it hit one of them.

GUIDO: What could it do to him? An empty shell? Forget

about it. *(Remembering now what Leone said, Guido seizes her passionately.)* Oh, darling, you're such a little baby!

SILIA: What?

GUIDO: Yes, that's how I want you! That's how you've got to be!

SILIA *(bursts out laughing)*: That's what he said!

GUIDO *(not put off, but with increasing passion, wanting her more and more)*: Yes, but it's true! It's true! Can't you see that in you there's a wild, adorable little child?

SILIA *(raising her hands as if to scratch him)*: I'm a tiger!

GUIDO *(still holding her)*: For him, yes. But I want you this way . . . a little baby . . .

SILIA *(teasingly)*: Then kill him for me!

GUIDO: Oh, go on! You don't know what you're saying.

SILIA *(childishly)*: If I'm going to be a naughty little girl, I can ask for anything I want.

GUIDO *(falling in with her joke)*: Because he's the big bad giant?

SILIA: Yes, and I'm so scared of him. Will you kill him for me? Please?

GUIDO: Yes, yes, I'll kill him for you, but first let's—

SILIA *(trying to break away)*: No, Guido, please . . .

GUIDO *(swept away)*: Can't you feel how I want you? All I have to do is touch you!

SILIA *(languidly)*: I said no . . .

GUIDO *(dragging her toward the bedroom)*: Yes, yes! Come on, Silia! I can't leave you now!

SILIA: No! Please! Let me alone!

GUIDO: Let you alone? No. I can't leave you!

SILIA: You know I don't want to. Not here. There's the maid . . .

(There's a knock at the door.)

You see?

GUIDO *(pushing her toward the door)*: Go and tell her not

to come in. I'll wait for you in there . . . *(exiting quickly)* . . . and hurry! *(He goes into the bedroom, closing the door behind him. Silia starts out when suddenly Clara's voice is heard.)*

CLARA *(shouting)*: Take your hands off me! Get out! She's not here!

(The door is pushed open and four men in evening dress, one of them the young Marquis Miglioriti, burst in, though Clara is still attempting to bar the way. They are all drunk.)

MIGLIORITI: Get out of the way, stupid! What do you mean she's not here? There she is!

FIRST DRUNK: Pepita darling!

SECOND DRUNK: *Viva l'España!*

THIRD DRUNK: And look at this place, gentlemen! *C'est charmant!*

SILIA: What is this? Who are they? How did they get in?

CLARA: They forced their way in! They're all drunk!

MIGLIORITI: What do you mean, forced?

FIRST DRUNK: Drunk? How dare you?

MIGLIORITI: You asked me up! You threw me a little present from the window!

SECOND DRUNK: We are four gay caballeros!

THIRD DRUNK *(going toward the dining room)*: How about a little something to drink for the nice customers? *Ah, c'est tout a fait delicieux!*

SILIA: Oh, God! What do they want?

CLARA: This is a respectable house!

MIGLIORITI: We know that, Pepita darling!

SILIA: Pepita?

CLARA: Yes, madam. The one who lives next door. I tried to tell them.

(Silia bursts out laughing, then stops abruptly. A strange light comes into her eyes, as if she has hit on a truly diabolical idea.)

SILIA: Ah, yes, gentlemen, of course! Pepita! Yes! I am Pepita!

SECOND DRUNK: *Viva l'España!*

SILIA: Yes, yes. Sit down, sit down. Or would you rather have a drink in there with your friend?

MIGLIORITI: No . . . I . . . I want something else! *(He grabs for her.)*

SILIA *(slipping coyly away)*: What would you like?

MIGLIORITI: You! I'll drink you!

SILIA: Not so fast! Wait! In a moment.

SECOND DRUNK: Me, too, Pepita!

SILIA *(defending herself)*: You, too? All right, but–easy now!

SECOND DRUNK: We'll do it the Spanish way!

FIRST DRUNK: You go ahead! I'll watch!

SILIA: Easy . . . easy now . . . there . . . first sit down . . . sit down, all of you . . . please . . . *(She pushes them aside, then leads them to various seats.)* Like that . . . good . . . there . . . like that . . . *(She runs to Clara and pulls her aside.)* Hurry up! Go get help! The neighbors . . . *(Clara nods and runs out.)*
Excuse me a moment. *(She goes to the bedroom door and locks it to keep Guido from entering.)*

MIGLIORITI *(trying to rise)*: Oh, if you have someone else in there, take your time, you know.

SECOND DRUNK: Yes, yes, we can wait.

FIRST DRUNK: I have no intention . . . but I'll watch.

SILIA: Now stay there, sit down . . . You gentlemen know exactly what you're doing, don't you?

ALL THREE: Perfectly! Of course we do! That's right!

SILIA: And you haven't any idea that this is a respectable house?

THIRD DRUNK *(returning from the dining room)*: *Oh, oui . . . mais . . . n'exagere pas, mon petit chou!* We want a little fun . . . *Voilà tout!*

SILIA: But I only entertain my friends. If you gentlemen would like to be friends . . .

SECOND DRUNK: What else?

FIRST DRUNK: Bosom friends!

SILIA: Then tell me who you are.

SECOND DRUNK: My name's Coco!

SILIA: No, not like that.

SECOND DRUNK: But it's true! I am Coco!

FIRST DRUNK: And I'm Meme!

SILIA: That isn't what I meant. Your real names. May I see your cards?

SECOND DRUNK: Ah, no, no, no! Thanks just the same, sweetheart!

FIRST DRUNK: I don't have one . . . I lost my wallet . . . *(To Miglioriti:)* Do me a favor. Give her one for me.

SILIA *(to Miglioriti)*: Yes, please. You're the nicest boy here.

MIGLIORITI *(taking out his wallet)*: No trouble at all.

SECOND DRUNK: His card is for all of us. *Voilà!*

MIGLIORITI: There you are, Pepita.

SILIA: Ah, thank you! That's very nice! So you're the Marquis Miglioriti?

FIRST DRUNK: The little marquis!

SILIA *(to Second Drunk)*: And you're Meme?

SECOND DRUNK: No, Coco. He's Meme. *(Indicating First Drunk.)*

SILIA: Fine. Coco . . . Meme. And you?

THIRD DRUNK *(with exaggerated cunning)*: *Moi . . . moi . . . je ne sais pas, mon petit chou!*

SILIA: It doesn't matter. I only need one of you.

SECOND DRUNK: But we'll all join in. We all want you—

THIRD DRUNK: The Spanish way!

FIRST DRUNK: I don't really care. I'll watch. But why don't you dance for us, Pepita? With castanets, you know?

SECOND DRUNK: Yes, first a little dance, then a little—

MIGLIORITI: But not all dressed up like that!

THIRD DRUNK: Not dressed at all, gentlemen! Take it off!

SECOND DRUNK *(throwing himself on Silia)*: That's right! Naked! Yes! Naked! Naked!

THE OTHERS *(also attacking her)*: Naked! Naked! Wonderful! Marvelous! Yes, naked!

SILIA *(twisting this way and that, finally breaking away)*: Not here, gentlemen, please! Naked, yes, but not here!

THIRD DRUNK: Where then?

SILIA: Why not in . . . in the piazza?

MIGLIORITI: The piazza?

SECOND DRUNK: What do you mean, the piazza?

FIRST DRUNK: Naked in the piazza?

SILIA: Why not? There's a lovely moon and no one else around. You should see how I look in the moonlight . . . naked. How about in front of the statue of the king on horseback? The four of you can sit there and I'll dance for you. And what a dance! And then— *(At this point Clara returns with the Neighbors, three men and two women, all shouting at once.)*

THE NEIGHBORS: What is it? What's going on? Who are they? Attacking her? Forced their way in? Where are they?

CLARA: There they are! There they are!

SILIA *(suddenly changing her whole attitude)*: Attacked! Attacked in my own home! They forced their way in, they tried to rape me! Look at my clothes! God knows what they would have done if you hadn't come!

SECOND MAN *(trying to shoo the drunks out)*: Out! Out!

FIRST MAN: Get away from her!

THIRD MAN: Get out of here!

FIRST DRUNK: Now, easy! Easy there!

SECOND MAN: Get out! Out!

FIRST WOMAN: Animals!

MIGLIORITI: We have a right to be here!

SECOND DRUNK: This Spanish stuff is for sale!

SECOND WOMAN: Shame on you!
FIRST WOMAN: Out, out, you drunks!
THIRD DRUNK: What's all the noise about anyway?
MIGLIORITI: Sweet Pepita here asked us up for a little party and–
SECOND MAN: Pepita? That's not Pepita!
FIRST WOMAN: Pepita indeed! That's Mrs. Gala.
THIRD MAN: Understand? Mrs. Leone Gala.
THE DRUNKS: Mrs. Gala?
FIRST MAN: That's right!
FIRST WOMAN: Shame on you!
SECOND DRUNK: Well, I see . . . then we made a mistake . . . We apologize.
THE NEIGHBORS: Out! Get out of here!
FIRST DRUNK: *Doucement, doucement, s'il vous plaît!*
MIGLIORITI: It was all his fault. He began to sing *Carmen.*
THIRD DRUNK: In honor of Spain.
THIRD MAN: That's enough now! Get out of here!
SECOND DRUNK: No. First we have to apologize to the lady.
FIRST MAN: This has gone far enough! Out with you!
MIGLIORITI: Ladies and gentlemen . . . please . . . all of you . . . on our knees we apologize . . . we beg the lady's pardon. *(He kneels.)*
SILIA: Oh, no! That's not enough, sir! I have your name! And you will answer for this outrage you and your friends have committed in my house!
MIGLIORITI: But if we apologize–
SILIA: I don't accept your apology and I won't listen to your excuses!
MIGLIORITI *(rising)*: Very well. You have my card. I'm at your disposal.
SILIA: Get out! Get out of my house this minute!
(The four drunks make a last effort to exit gracefully, but they are chased out by the Neighbors and shown the door by Clara.)

(To the Neighbors:) Thank you very much for coming and I'm so sorry to have disturbed you.

SECOND MAN: Not at all, Mrs. Gala.

FIRST MAN: Our duty, our duty!

FIRST WOMAN: After all, we're your neighbors.

THIRD MAN: Those swine!

FIRST WOMAN: We're not safe even in our own homes!

SECOND WOMAN: Perhaps, however, Mrs. Gala might now forgive . . . I mean, they did apologize.

SILIA: Oh, no, I'm very sorry! I told them again and again that they were in a respectable house and they still— You can't imagine what they said to me!

FIRST MAN: Mrs. Gala is absolutely right!

SECOND MAN: Of course she is! Absolutely!

BOTH WOMEN: A lesson! They need a lesson! The poor woman!

SILIA: I know who one of these—these so-called gentlemen is. Imagine! He gave me his card to show me that, if this were a respectable house, he was every inch a gentleman!

THIRD MAN: Who is he? Who is he?

SILIA: There! Read it! The Marquis Miglioriti!

FIRST WOMAN: Oh! The Marquis Miglioriti!

SECOND WOMAN: A marquis!

ALL: Shame on him! Shame!

SILIA: You see my position?

SECOND WOMAN: Of course! She's right! They need a lesson!

FIRST WOMAN: They ought to be exposed!

THIRD MAN: And punished!

FIRST MAN: In front of the whole town!

SECOND MAN: Now try to calm yourself, Mrs. Gala.

SECOND WOMAN: Yes, get some rest.

FIRST WOMAN: We'll leave you now.

ALL *(exiting)*: Good-by . . . Good-by . . . Good night . . .

(As soon as they've gone, Silia, flushed with joy, exultant, looks at Miglioriti's card and gestures triumphantly, having apparently achieved her secret purpose. Meanwhile, Guido is pounding on the bedroom door.)

SILIA: All right, I'm coming! I'm coming! *(She runs to let him out.)*

GUIDO *(entering in a great rage)*: Why did you lock me in? I nearly chewed my hands off, I was so angry!

SILIA: That's all I needed! To have you come out of my bedroom in front of four witnesses and . . . *(looking at him out of wild, laughing eyes)* . . . and ruin everything! *(Showing Guido the marquis's card.)* Look! I have it! Here it is!

GUIDO: I know. I know the man well. What are you up to?

SILIA: Here it is, I tell you! For Leone!

GUIDO *(frightened)*: Silia! *(He goes toward her to take away the card.)*

SILIA *(avoiding him)*: What? Don't you want to see if I can't cause him just a little bit of trouble?

GUIDO: Do you know who that man is?

SILIA: The Marquis Aldo Miglioriti.

GUIDO: Then for heaven's sake, Silia, get the idea out of your head!

SILIA: I will not get the idea out of my head! My husband leaves me here with a lover incapable of protecting me, to be insulted and nearly raped by four drunks! Now it's up to him to do something!

GUIDO: Silia, I'm not going to let you get away with it.

SILIA: How are you going to stop me? You can't stop me!

GUIDO: We'll see about that.

SILIA: Yes, we'll see! Tomorrow! *(Imperiously, haughtily.)* Now listen, Guido, that's enough! I'm very tired!

GUIDO *(darkly, threateningly)*: I'm going, Silia.

SILIA: No! *(Changing mood abruptly, soft and gentle now.)* Come here . . .

GUIDO *(suspiciously)*: What do you want?

SILIA: I want . . . I want . . . I want you to be nice to me . . . *(A pause, then she laughs.)* Those poor boys! I was really very mean to them!

GUIDO: Yes, that's exactly what I wanted to tell you. You had no right to be.

SILIA *(cutting him off disdainfully)*: I don't want to discuss it, if you don't mind.

GUIDO: They made a mistake and they apologized for it.

SILIA: That's enough, I said! I don't want to talk about it! *(A pause.)* All I meant was . . . they were so funny . . . *(With a sigh of deeply felt envy.)* Isn't it strange . . . the things men can think of at night . . . They wanted to see me dance, you know . . . in the piazza . . . by moonlight . . . *(then, very softly, almost in his ear:)* . . . naked! . . .

GUIDO: Silia . . .

(Silia suddenly lowers her head and shakes her curls in his face.)

SILIA: Oh, I'm your naughty little baby!

CURTAIN

ACT II

Leone's house, late the following morning; a strange combination of dining room and studio. Leone, comically attired in a chef's hat and apron, is busily beating some sort of an egg sauce in a bowl. Filippo, also dressed up as a chef, is similarly occupied. Guido is sitting in a chair, listening to their conversation.

LEONE *(to Guido, alluding to Filippo)*: Isn't he delightful? My guardian demon!

FILIPPO: Yes, straight from hell!

LEONE: Such language! That's hardly the way I'd expect—

FILIPPO: Why don't you keep quiet?

LEONE: —expect a Socrates to talk!

FILIPPO: I'm sick of hearing about this Socrates! Anyway, I don't know him!

LEONE: What? You don't know him?

FILIPPO: No. And, furthermore, I don't want to! Watch what you're doing!

LEONE: I am, I am.

FILIPPO: Not that way!

LEONE: What?

FILIPPO: The spoon! The spoon!

LEONE: I'm doing it right! Stop worrying!

FILIPPO: You'll poison the poor man's lunch, if you don't stop talking.

GUIDO: No, no. I'm enjoying myself immensely.

LEONE: There's nothing like a little metaphysical conversation to whet the appetite.

FILIPPO: Well, I find it very distracting.

LEONE: Ah, that's why you're upset!

FILIPPO: Of course, of course . . . Now what are you doing?

LEONE: What am I doing?

FILIPPO: Go on beating the egg, for God's sake! It will never set if you keep stopping all the time!

LEONE: All right, all right.

FILIPPO: How can I be expected to get anything done when I have to keep one eye on what he's doing and both ears open to what he says, while my head spins with all the absurdities he spouts? I'm going to the kitchen!

LEONE: Oh, come, Filippo! It's all right. Stay here. I promise to keep quiet. *(Softly to Guido, but loud enough for Filippo to overhear:)* Bergson's philosophy has ruined him.

FILIPPO: Now he's going to start in on this Bergson!

LEONE: But of course! *(To Guido:)* From the moment I exposed him to Bergson's theory of intuition, he's changed completely. He used to be a formidable thinker.

FILIPPO: You know perfectly well I've never had a thought in my head! And I'll prove it to you immediately if you go on like this. I'll drop everything and walk out of here once and forever!

LEONE: You see? And then I'm not supposed to say that Bergson ruined him for me! As for Bergson himself, well, it's possible, I suppose, to find some merit in his criticism of the rational mind.

FILIPPO: Please! Enough! Beat your egg!

LEONE: I am, I am. But listen to this, Guido! Bergson claims that everything fluid, alive, inconstant, and mysterious in life escapes the grasp of intellect. How it escapes I don't know, if only because Mr. Bergson is able to say so. How did he arrive at such a conclusion, if not by using his mind? In which case it hasn't escaped at all, has it?

FILIPPO *(shouting)*: Beat your egg!

LEONE: I am, can't you see? Now listen, Guido: this is a magnificent joke Bergson's mind has played on him! He sets intuition above intellect, because only intuition, deriving from instinct, perceives the reality of time, the secret of the life force. The intellect, he says, only understands matter, everything that is divisible and measurable. But—

(During this speech Filippo has never for a moment taken his eyes off Leone. Still beating his own egg, he quietly, stealthily creeps up on Leone, waiting until the

latter, carried away by his own eloquence, again forgets to beat his egg, at which point . . .)

FILIPPO *(shouting)*: And now what are you doing?

LEONE *(starting, then hastily resuming)*: You're right, you're right! I'll pay attention.

FILIPPO: Can't you see that all this talk about the intellect is only driving you out of your mind?

LEONE: Now listen—as if beating an egg is all my mind is good for! Have a little patience. I recognize the necessity of beating eggs and I bow to this necessity you taught me. However—

GUIDO: You're really divine, both of you!

LEONE: Not at all. Only I am divine. He, corrupted by Bergson—

FILIPPO: I tell you no one has corrupted me!

LEONE: You're wrong, my friend. You've become so deplorably human I don't even know you any more. Let me talk a little bit, for God's sake! In any case, I've finished with this.

(As Leone sets the bowl down, the doorbell rings. Filippo also puts his bowl down and starts off to open the door.) Wait a minute. First come here and get me out of this thing. *(Filippo goes to him and helps him out of the apron.)* And take this into the kitchen, too. *(Leone removes his hat and hands it to Filippo.)*

FILIPPO *(sarcastically)*: You've certainly done it honor! *(Filippo exits into the kitchen where he leaves Leone's hat and apron, then re-enters to remove the bowls, forgetting to go and open the door. The ensuing dialogue between Leone and Guido moves very rapidly.)*

GUIDO *(who has risen in alarm at the sound of the bell)*: Did . . . did someone ring?

LEONE: Yes. What's the matter?

GUIDO: Oh, God, Leone! It's Silia!

LEONE: Silia? Here?

GUIDO: Yes. Listen! Please! I originally came here this morning to—to warn you!

LEONE: To warn me?

GUIDO: Something happened last night—

LEONE: To Silia?

GUIDO: It was nothing, really. A trifle. I didn't even mention it to you because I was hoping she'd sleep on it and forget all about it. *(The doorbell rings again, more insistently this time.)* And now here she is! Oh, God, it must be she!

LEONE *(calmly turning toward the kitchen)*: Socrates, in there! Go and open the door!

GUIDO: Wait! Wait! *(To Filippo as he enters:)* Wait a moment!

FILIPPO: I completely forgot. *(He starts for the door.)*

GUIDO: Just a minute! Please! *(To Leone:)* I'm warning you, Leone, your wife is about to do something insane!

LEONE: That's nothing new.

GUIDO: And she wants to involve you!

LEONE: Me? Oh. *(To Filippo:)* Let her in, Filippo, let her in. *(To Guido:)* For this very reason, my dear Guido, my wife's visits are always most welcome.

(Filippo, more annoyed than ever, goes to answer the door.)

GUIDO: But you don't know what it's all about.

LEONE: It doesn't matter. Let her try. You'll see: I'll catch it, punch a hole in each end and suck it up!

(Silia enters like a cyclone, followed by Filippo who immediately exits into the kitchen, and sees Guido.)

SILIA: Ah! You here? You came to warn him?

GUIDO: No, Silia, I swear it. I've told him nothing.

SILIA *(turning on Leone:)* He knows! I can tell!

LEONE: No, my dear. Nothing. *(Teasingly, lightly.)* Good morning.

SILIA: Never mind that good-morning business! *(To Guido, menacingly:)* If you did . . .

LEONE: No, no. You can speak with absolute confidence in achieving the maximum effect of astonishment you've been anticipating. He hasn't told me a thing. Better still, why don't you go out and make your entrance all over again? I promise to be taken by surprise.

SILIA: I warn you, Leone, this is no laughing matter! *(To Guido:)* What are you doing here then?

GUIDO: Well . . . I came . . . I . . .

LEONE: Tell her the truth. To warn me, it's true, that you're up to something foolish.

SILIA: I am, am I?

GUIDO: Yes, you most certainly are!

LEONE: But he hasn't told me what it is. I haven't the faintest idea.

GUIDO: I was hoping you wouldn't go through with it—

LEONE: And so he hasn't told me anything, understand? Nothing!

SILIA: Then how do you know I'm acting foolishly?

LEONE: Oh, I could have guessed that all by myself. Although he did say—

GUIDO: Yes, I told him that much. It's insane! And I'll say it again!

SILIA *(in stentorian tones, at the end of her patience)*: Keep quiet! You haven't any right to judge my feelings! *(A pause, then turning to Leone and firing the words at him.)* You've been challenged to a duel!

LEONE: I have?

GUIDO: No, no . . .

SILIA: Yes, you have! You have!

LEONE: By whom?

GUIDO: It's absurd, Leone. She—

SILIA: Yes, challenged! I'm not sure whether he challenged

you or if it's up to you to challenge him. I don't know about such things. Anyway, I have the wretch's card here somewhere. *(Taking the card out of her purse.)* Here it is! *(She hands it to Leone.)* Get dressed at once and go find some people to represent you.

LEONE: Now just a minute—

SILIA: No! At once! I want you to go at once! And don't listen to him! He wants you to think I'm behaving like an idiot because it suits his purpose.

LEONE: Ah, it does?

GUIDO *(indignantly)*: It does nothing of the kind! What purpose are you talking about?

SILIA: It does! It does! You would have pardoned him on the spot—that swine!

LEONE *(looking at the card)*: But who is he?

GUIDO: The Marquis Aldo Miglioriti.

LEONE: You know him?

GUIDO: Very well. He's one of the best swordsmen in the country.

SILIA: Ah, so *that's* the reason!

GUIDO *(pale, trembling)*: What do you mean that's the reason? What are you insinuating?

SILIA *(almost to herself, with contempt and scorn)*: That's why . . . That's why . . .

LEONE: Now, will someone please tell me what happened? Why I've been challenged? Or why I should be expected to challenge anyone?

SILIA *(exploding)*: Because I've been insulted, insulted, and violently attacked, nearly raped in my own home! Because of you! I was left alone, defenseless! They put their dirty hands all over me, pawing me . . . here . . . here . . . on my breasts! Understand? And it was all your fault! They thought I was a— Oh! *(She covers her face with her hands and bursts into dry sobs of rage and shame.)*

LEONE: But who? You mean this Marquis—

SILIA: There were four of them. You saw them.

LEONE: Ah, the four young men who were standing by the front door when I left?

SILIA: Yes, that's who it was. They came up, they forced their way in—

GUIDO: But they were drunk! They didn't know what they were doing!

LEONE: What? You were there?

(At this question, delivered in a tone of astonishment, Silia and Guido break off in confusion.)

GUIDO: Yes . . . but . . . I wasn't . . . I mean . . .

SILIA *(returning immediately to the attack)*: What did you expect? That he would defend me? Do you think it was up to him? When my own husband had just turned his back on me, abandoning me to the brutal advances of a gang of sex maniacs! Why, if he had even shown himself—

GUIDO: I was in the other room.

SILIA *(hastily)*: The dining room.

LEONE: Having another little glass of liqueur?

SILIA *(furiously)*: Do you know what they said to me? "If you have someone else in there, take your time!" Can you imagine? That's all I needed; to have him stick his nose in and ruin my reputation completely! My God, my God, what a disaster! Luckily, he understood the situation.

LEONE: I see . . . I see . . . But I'm amazed, Silia—no, not amazed—I'm actually stupefied, my dear, that that lovely little head was capable of making such a subtle distinction.

SILIA *(puzzled)*: What distinction?

LEONE: Why, that it was up to me to defend you, because I am the husband, you are the wife, and he is the— Well, it goes without saying that if he had burst in and shown himself to those four drunken hoodlums, especially as he, too, must have been a little drunk—

GUIDO: I was not! I swear to you, Leone, I was only being discreet!

LEONE: And you were absolutely right, my boy! But isn't it miraculous, simply miraculous, that this lovely little head immediately understood that you were being discreet, that you would have compromised her by showing yourself? And so she didn't scream for help, not even when she was being attacked by four grown men—

SILIA *(in a tiny, helpless voice)*: Who actually tried to rape me, you know? All four of them—their hands all over me—tearing at my clothes—

LEONE *(to Guido)*: Hear that? And she thought of me! She understood that it was up to me to defend her! This is such a miracle of spontaneous insight that I at once step forward—yes, at once, at once!—and proclaim myself more than ready to do everything expected of me!

SILIA *(hardly daring to believe her ears)*: Ah! Good!

GUIDO: What? You accept?

LEONE *(smiling)*: Of course I accept! I have no choice. You're not making much sense, Guido.

GUIDO *(amazed)*: I'm not making sense?

LEONE: No. Can't you see that my acceptance is the direct consequence of your discretion?

SILIA *(triumphantly)*: It's true! He's right! *(She claps her hands with delight.)*

GUIDO *(confused)*: How? What does my being discreet have to do with it?

LEONE: Think about it a little. If she has been the victim of such an outrageous attack and you were right to be so discreet, then it's perfectly clear that I must be the one to do the actual challenging!

GUIDO: No, not at all! I don't see that at all! Because my

discretion was motivated by . . . well . . . because I knew they didn't know what they were doing—

SILIA *(exploding)*: That's not true!

GUIDO *(to Leone)*: You understand: they were drunk, they mistook the address, and later they apologized.

SILIA: I didn't accept their apology! Convenient, isn't it, to have your fun first and apologize later? I couldn't accept it! And listen to him—talking as if they'd apologized to him! As if he had gone through it all, instead of hiding in the other room!

LEONE *(to Guido)*: You see? Now you're spoiling everything, dear boy!

SILIA: I was the one who suffered!

LEONE *(to Guido)*: She was the one! *(To Silia:)* And at once you thought of your husband, isn't that so? *(To Guido:)* I'm sorry, Guido, but obviously you haven't thought this out very clearly!

GUIDO *(exasperated)*: Oh, leave me alone! What is there to think out?

LEONE: Well, look at it this way: You were right—yes, absolutely right—to say that you would have compromised her by interfering, but not because they were drunk. If anything, that would be an excuse for me not to challenge them, for me not to have to call them to account.

SILIA *(disappointed)*: Oh? Why not?

LEONE: I said "if anything." Don't worry, Silia. *(To Guido:)* But their being drunk is no excuse for you, Guido. I mean, if they were that drunk, you could very easily have been a little less cautious.

SILIA: True! Very true! With drunks . . . And then you were only paying me a social visit. It wasn't even midnight.

GUIDO *(angrily)*: That isn't so! And you just said that I—

LEONE *(quickly, turning to Silia)*: No, no, no, please! He

was right not to interfere, Silia. You said so yourself. Just as you were right to think of me. In fact, you've both been very right!

GUIDO *(caught between two fires)*: But no . . . but I . . .

LEONE: Stop worrying about it, Guido. I couldn't be more delighted that for the first time in her life Silia has found a concept to stand on. Imagine! She has understood that I am trapped in my assigned role of husband. And I haven't the slightest intention of disillusioning her. *(To Silia:)* Yes, my darling, yes, I am the husband and you are the wife and he—well, naturally he will act as my second.

GUIDO: Oh, no! Not a chance! You can just forget about that!

LEONE: Why?

GUIDO: Because I don't accept!

LEONE: You don't accept?

GUIDO: No!

LEONE: But you have to accept.

GUIDO: I told you to forget about it. I don't accept.

SILIA *(bitingly)*: He's being discreet again.

GUIDO *(exasperated)*: Now listen, Silia—

LEONE *(placatingly)*: Please, please, my friends. Let's talk it out calmly. *(To Guido:)* Guido, I don't see how you can refuse me. You've been involved in several of these affairs before and you know the correct procedure. I haven't any idea what I'm supposed to do. And everybody knows you're a close friend of mine. What would people say if I had to turn elsewhere for help?

GUIDO: I don't care what they'd say! That's what you'll have to do, because I will not be your second.

LEONE *(gazing steadily at him)*: In that case, you'll have to give me a good reason. And you can't. *(Amiably.)* Now, you know you can't justify such a refusal, either to me or to anyone else.

GUIDO: What do you mean I can't? As far as I'm concerned, there's no reason to have a duel at all!

LEONE: That's not for you to decide.

SILIA: It was I who refused the man's apology! And in front of everybody!

LEONE: Ah, there were other witnesses?

SILIA: Yes. My screams woke up the neighbors. They all said those men ought to be taught a lesson!

LEONE *(to Guido)*: You see? A public scandal! *(To Silia:)* You're right, of course. *(To Guido again:)* Come on, Guido, it's useless to discuss it any further.

GUIDO *(giving up, partly in order to ingratiate himself again with Silia)*: Oh, all right! If you insist on being led to the slaughter, why should I care?

SILIA *(nervously)*: Now, Guido, let's not exaggerate!

GUIDO: I'm not. A slaughter is exactly what it will be. But if he wants to get himself killed, I'm not going to stand in his way.

LEONE: No, really, it's not up to me. It's what you two want that counts.

SILIA: But there's no need to fight a real duel. Hardly anybody does that any more. It's only a formality, isn't it?

GUIDO: No, I'm sorry, Silia. In this case there are only two choices: either we fight a duel or we don't. If there is to be a duel at all, then it will have to be a real one and fought under the most serious conditions.

LEONE: Oh, undoubtedly, undoubtedly.

SILIA: But why?

GUIDO: Because if I go and deliver Leone's challenge, it means I'm ignoring the fact that these people were all drunk–

LEONE: Absolutely correct.

GUIDO: In which case their behavior in your house becomes a most serious matter.

LEONE: Obviously.

SILIA: Then it's up to you to treat the situation lightly.

GUIDO: I can't! How do you expect me to do that?

LEONE: You're quite right. *(To Silia:)* He can't do that.

GUIDO: Also, when Miglioriti finds out that no consideration is being given to the fact that he was drunk at the time and that all his attempts to apologize have been rejected–

LEONE: Yes, of course.

GUIDO: To get even, you understand.

LEONE: It's only natural.

GUIDO: He will insist on a real duel!

LEONE *(chuckling)*: Yes, he's sure to make that an excuse to fight a good one! The eager rascal!

GUIDO: You'd better do some thinking about it, Leone. As I told you, he's one of the best fencers I've ever seen. And you, you don't even know which end of the sword to hold.

LEONE: You're quite right, but that's your department. Why should I bother about such things?

GUIDO: What do you mean, it's my department?

LEONE: Well, I'm certainly not going to worry about it.

GUIDO: But do you understand my responsibility?

LEONE: Certainly. It's a very serious one, I know. I'm sorry for you. But you have to act out your role in life, just as I have to act out mine. That's how the game is played, my friend. Even she finally understands. We must each play our parts to the hilt, right to the end. And you can both rest assured that from where I stand I will not budge an inch, no matter what happens. We're all going to play this little game together and it's certain to be entertaining. So that's that.

(The doorbell rings again. Filippo, still furious, enters and goes to answer it.)

All I want now is to get it over with quickly. Go and

take care of everything, Guido . . . Oh, do you need any money?

GUIDO: No, not right now.

LEONE: I suppose it will be expensive: the witnesses, the police, and so on.

GUIDO: Yes, but there's plenty of time.

LEONE: All right, we'll settle up later.

GUIDO: How do you feel about the fencing master, Barelli, as a witness?

LEONE: Fine, fine. Barelli or anyone else . . .
(Seeing Spiga enter, followed by Filippo.)
Come in, come in, Spiga. *(To Guido:)* And while we're at it, Guido, here's our medical expert. You know Dr. Spiga.

GUIDO: Yes. Good morning, Doctor.

LEONE: If you have confidence in him . . .

GUIDO: Really, I–

LEONE: He's good, you know. One of our most distinguished surgeons. But I wouldn't want to inconvenience him too much, so I was wondering . . . *(Noticing that Guido has turned away to say something to Silia.)* Guido! Listen to me! This place is very isolated –I live out here like a hermit–and there's a small vegetable garden in back of the house. We could get the whole thing over with right here, early tomorrow morning.

GUIDO: Yes, yes. Fine. Now, if you'll please stop delaying me, I'll go and make all the arrangements. *(He squeezes Silia's hand and bows to Spiga.)* Doctor . . . *(To Leone:)* I'll see you soon, Leone . . . No, wait. I have quite a lot to do. I'd better send you Barelli first. I'll come back this evening. Good-by. *(He exits quickly.)*

SPIGA: What's going on, if I may ask?

LEONE: Come here, come here, Spiga. I'd like to introduce you to my wife.

SPIGA: Oh? Really?

LEONE *(to Silia)*: My dear, this is Dr. Spiga—my friend, neighbor, and fearless contradictor!

SPIGA: I'm delighted, Mrs. Gala . . . Then this is a . . . Ah, I congratulate you both, even though it means that I shall perhaps lose the pleasure of a company to which I have become more than merely accustomed.

LEONE: No, no, Spiga. What do you think is happening here?

SPIGA: Isn't this a reconciliation?

LEONE: No, my friend, nothing like that. We're not separated at all. We live in perfect harmony—apart.

SPIGA: Ah . . . I see . . . I beg your pardon . . . Yes, I was about to say . . . that is, I was wondering what my being a surgeon had to do with your getting together again. It did seem a little strange, if you know what I mean.

FILIPPO *(unable any longer to contain himself)*: Strange? Strange? Doctor, in this house nothing is strange! You're lucky you didn't have to operate on the spot! Nothing too absurd, nothing too mad can possibly happen here! But I won't stand for it any longer! I'm going! Today! At once! This instant! *(Gesturing furiously, he exits into the kitchen.)*

LEONE *(to Spiga)*: Go in there and say something soothing. See if you can't calm him down. Bergson, Bergson, my dear fellow! A disastrous effect! *(Spiga laughs. Then, as Leone pushes him toward the kitchen, he turns back.)*

SPIGA: With your permission, Mrs. Gala. *(To Leone:)* But I still don't see what my surgery has to do with anything.

LEONE: Go on, go on. He'll explain it to you.

SPIGA: Uhm. *(He exits.)*

(Leone goes behind the chair in which Silia, absorbed in her own thoughts, is sitting, then bends over to look at her.)

LEONE *(softly, tenderly)*: Well? Are you going to just sit there, like a statue? Why so silent?

SILIA *(forcing herself to speak)*: I . . . I never dreamed that . . . that you would—

LEONE: That I would what?

SILIA: That you would say yes.

LEONE: You know very well I've always said yes to you, Silia.

(Silia suddenly jumps to her feet. She is a prey to her conflicting emotions: irritation at the passive docility of her husband, remorse for her own actions, and, lastly, contempt for her lover, because he first tried to duck any responsibility and then, in an effort to ingratiate himself with her, shows signs of going too far.)

SILIA: I can't stand it! I can't stand it! *(She is on the verge of tears.)*

LEONE *(pretending not to understand)*: What? That I said yes?

SILIA: Not only that! It's . . . it's everything! All this . . . this . . . Well, you're to blame that he's taking advantage of the situation.

LEONE: I'm to blame?

SILIA: Yes! Yes, of course you are! Because of your unforgivable, absolutely impossible indifference!

LEONE: Do you mean my indifference now, to this particular situation, or do you mean my attitude in general, as it pertains . . . to you?

SILIA: I meant in general. Yes, to everything, always! But especially now!

LEONE: Do you really think Guido is taking advantage of it?

SILIA: Couldn't you tell? At first he wanted no part of it, but then, when he saw how docile you were, he changed his mind. God knows what conditions he'll impose!

LEONE: Aren't you being a little unjust?

SILIA: I told him to go and treat the matter lightly with Miglioriti. There's no need to exaggerate the affair.

LEONE: Perhaps not, but it was you who pushed him into it in the first place.

SILIA: Because he wouldn't do what I wanted him to.

LEONE: Yes, very true. He didn't think your reasons were very sound.

SILIA: And you?

LEONE: And I what?

SILIA: What do you think?

LEONE: Can't you tell? I agreed to everything.

SILIA: Yes, but I suppose you think I also exaggerated.

LEONE: You indicated to Guido, and I think you were correct, that no one has any right to judge the feelings of others.

SILIA: Oh, Leone, maybe I did exaggerate the incident a little, but it was his fault if I did!

LEONE: Yes, because he wouldn't give in to you.

SILIA: And for that very reason he has no business making *my* exaggeration a pretext for *his* exaggeration!

LEONE: Well, Silia, you pushed him pretty hard. He has feelings, too. You've both exaggerated a little, that's all.

SILIA *(after a pause, during which she looks at him in amazement)*: And you? Still so calm? So indifferent?

LEONE: You must allow me to defend myself the only way I know, the only way I can.

SILIA: You think your indifference will protect you this time?

LEONE: Oh, yes. Most certainly.

SILIA: Even if the man is as skillful a swordsman as Guido says he is?

LEONE: I'll let my able second worry about that. Why should I care?

SILIA: You don't even know how to hold a sword.

LEONE: I don't need to. You can be certain, Silia, that my

indifference will be enough to make me unafraid, not just of a single man armed with a sword, which is nothing, but of all men everywhere, and for always. I live in a climate, my dear, where nothing can touch me, where life and death have no significance. Imagine, then, whether I care for the petty judgments and entanglements of a ridiculous world. Don't worry about me, Silia. I understand the game.

FILIPPO *(shouting from inside the kitchen)*: Why don't you go naked?

SPIGA *(entering)*: Naked? Are you mad? *(To Leone:)* The man's a fiend, damn him! Oh, I . . . I beg your pardon, Mrs. Gala.

LEONE *(laughing)*: What's the matter?

SPIGA: Leone, what *is* going on here? Are you really involved in a duel? You?

LEONE: Incredible, isn't it?

SPIGA *(somewhat embarrassed, eying Silia)*: Yes . . . I mean, no . . . but . . . excuse me, Mrs. Gala . . . it's just that I . . . Well, I couldn't make out what the devil that madman in there was talking about. You've actually challenged somebody to a duel?

LEONE: Yes, indeed.

SPIGA: But why?

LEONE: I had no choice. They insulted my wife.

SPIGA: Oh, I'm so sorry, Mrs. Gala. It's really none of my business, I know, but . . . *(turning back to Leone)* . . . it's just that I . . . you understand . . . I've . . . I've never attended a duel before.

LEONE: Well, that makes two of us. So we're even. It will be a new experience for both of us.

SPIGA: Yes, but . . . I mean . . . the formalities, you see. What . . . what should I wear, for instance?

LEONE *(laughing)*: Oh, now I understand. That's what you were asking Socrates in the kitchen.

SPIGA: He told me to go naked! I . . . I wouldn't want to make a fool of myself.

LEONE: My poor friend! I haven't any idea what attending physicians at duels are expected to wear. But don't worry, we'll ask Guido. He's always up on current fashions.

SPIGA: And . . . and I suppose I should bring my instruments, shouldn't I?

(Filippo enters.)

LEONE: Certainly.

SPIGA *(indicating Filippo)*: It's . . . it's going to be a real duel, he says.

LEONE: So it seems.

SPIGA: With real swords?

LEONE: Apparently.

SPIGA: Do you think my regular bag will be enough?

LEONE: Listen: it's going to be fought in back of the house, over my spinach, so you can bring your whole armory, if you like.

SPIGA: Excellent! Excellent! That will be most convenient.

(The doorbell rings. Filippo goes to answer it.)

SILIA: Is that Guido? Back already?

SPIGA: Guido? Ah, splendid! Then I can ask him . . .

(Filippo returns and goes toward the kitchen.)

LEONE: Who is it?

FILIPPO *(loudly, rudely)*: How should I know? Some imbecile armed to the teeth! *(He stamps angrily into the kitchen. Barelli now appears in the doorway. He is carrying a large sword case and a brace of pistols.)*

BARELLI: May I come in?

LEONE: Of course, of course, Barelli. We've been expecting you. What's the arsenal for?

BARELLI *(very excited)*: Leone, have you gone mad? The whole thing's insane, idiotic! You can't—

(Leone has been gesturing toward Silia.)

What? What is it?

LEONE: I want you to meet my wife. *(To Silia:)* My dear, this is the incomparable Barelli.

BARELLI *(bowing)*: My pleasure.

LEONE: And this is Dr. Spiga.

SPIGA *(shaking Barelli's hand and holding on)*: Delighted! Delighted! *(Turning to Leone.)* Now?

LEONE: No. Later, later.

BARELLI: I tell you, I've never seen anything like it! It's absolutely incredible! What do you think this is, Leone? The eighteenth century? It's fantastic! *(To Silia:)* I'm sorry, Mrs. Gala, but if I don't say what I think, I'll explode! *(To Leone again:)* What are you doing? How dare you send an unconditional challenge?

LEONE: What does that mean? Explain yourself.

BARELLI: What? You issued the challenge and you don't know what it means?

LEONE: Why should I bother about such trivialities?

BARELLI: Trivialities?

SILIA: What kind of challenge?

SPIGA: Unconditional, you say?

BARELLI: It means there's no hope for a settlement or a compromise of any kind. Why, it's unheard of! No one fights that kind of duel any more! It's illegal, it's immoral, it's—it's impossible! And the conditions! My God, Leone, why don't you just fire cannons at each other and get it over with?

SPIGA: Cannons?

SILIA: What do you mean?

BARELLI: First these maniacs will bang away with pistols . . .

SILIA: Pistols?

LEONE *(to Silia)*: Probably Guido's idea. The marquis is too good a fencer. With a gun, perhaps—

BARELLI: Have you ever seen him shoot? No? I have. He'll knock the wings off a butterfly at fifty paces.

SILIA: And using pistols was Guido's idea?

BARELLI: Oh, yes! He insisted! He must be out of his mind!

SILIA *(to Leone)*: I told you!

SPIGA: Excuse me, but where does this butterfly come in?

BARELLI: What butterfly?

LEONE *(to Spiga)*: Never mind, never mind, my friend. These are things you and I know nothing about.

BARELLI: They will begin by firing two shots apiece at each other. Then, if they survive that barrage, they will have a chance to use their swords!

SILIA: Swords, too! You hear that? You hear? The pistols weren't enough for him! He wanted swords as well!

BARELLI: Not quite accurate, madam. They had already agreed upon the swords when Guido suggested the pistols as a sort of happy afterthought. He seemed to think it was a huge joke! "Literally playing with fire" was the delightful way he put it, I believe!

SILIA: But this is murder!

BARELLI: I quite agree. But it was up to you to stop it.

SILIA: Up to me? How? He'll tell you I did my best. *(She indicates Leone.)*

LEONE: Oh, yes, she did her very best.

SILIA: I certainly never wanted it to go this far. Isn't there anything we can do?

BARELLI: Well—

LEONE *(sharply, to Barelli)*: That's enough, Barelli! I'm sorry, but I can see no point in discussing it any further, especially with her.

BARELLI: But . . . but you don't know what's happening! It's all over the city! No one talks of anything else! And they say—

SILIA: That I'm to blame? Is that what they think?

BARELLI: No, not you, Mrs. Gala! It's Guido! *(To Leone:)* You understand, Leone, no one says anything against either of you. Your name isn't even mentioned. It's Guido's behavior that shocks everyone. And Miglioriti is absolutely furious with him. You see, everybody knows he was there when it happened; he admits it himself. And apparently he did nothing to stop it. Nothing. They say he was afraid, but I can't believe that. After all, Miglioriti and the others were very drunk. He could have easily handled the situation, although I know that at school they were rivals in everything. But no! He hides! He makes no attempt to avoid an ugly scandal! And then, to top it all off, he has the nerve to confront Miglioriti with your challenge. Why, it's . . . it's incredible! I . . . I don't even know where I am any more!

SPIGA *(to Leone)*: Listen, Leone, perhaps I could—

LEONE *(sharply)*: Keep out of things you don't understand, my friend!

SPIGA: All I wanted was to . . . I mean, since you are planning to hold it nearby . . .

BARELLI: Yes, in the garden. Tomorrow morning, at seven o'clock. Look, Leone, I brought along a couple of swords . . .

LEONE *(pretending not to understand)*: You want me to pay for them?

BARELLI: Pay for them? Of course not! They're mine. I thought I could give you a few pointers, let you get the feel of it.

LEONE: Why me?

BARELLI: Well, who else? It's not for my benefit!

LEONE *(laughing)*: No, no, no. Never mind. It's quite unnecessary.

BARELLI: What do you mean it's unnecessary? *(He picks up*

one of the swords and begins to flourish it about.) I'll bet you don't even know how to hold one. Look! *En garde!*

SILIA *(frightened)*: Don't! Please!

LEONE: That's enough, Barelli. The joke is wearing a little thin.

BARELLI: Joke? I'm not joking. You at least ought to learn how to hold it.

LEONE: And I said that's enough! More than enough! I say it to you and to everyone here. I want to be left alone! Is that clear?

BARELLI: All right, Leone. I—I see your point. You should certainly have some peace and quiet. And do try to keep calm.

LEONE: Don't worry about me, Barelli. I'm always calm. But this is becoming something of a bore. I need a little breathing space, that's all. If you want to play with your toys, you can do that tonight, when Guido comes, and while you big brave fellows slash away at each other, I'll stand by and watch. Fair enough? Until then just leave them there and please don't be offended if I ask you to go now.

BARELLI: Oh, as far as I'm concerned, you can do what you like.

LEONE: And you, too, Doctor, please.

SPIGA: Of course, of course!

LEONE: He'll tell you everything you want to know.

BARELLI *(bowing to Silia)*: Madam . . .

(Silia nods to him.)

SPIGA: My dear Mrs. Gala. *(He shakes her hand. To Leone:)* Till later, eh? Now keep calm, Leone, keep calm.

LEONE: Of course. Good-by.

BARELLI: I'll be back this evening, Leone.

LEONE: Fine, fine. Good-by, Barelli.

(Spiga and Barelli exit.)

LEONE: Ah, thank God! What a relief! I couldn't have stood another minute of it!

SILIA: I'll go, too . . .

LEONE: No, please. Stay, if you like. As long as you don't mention this tedious business again.

SILIA: That wouldn't be possible, Leone. And then I . . . I don't want to be here when Guido comes back. I don't know what I'd do to him. I . . . I wouldn't trust myself. *(Leone laughs heartily.)*
Don't laugh! Don't laugh!

LEONE: I can't help it, Silia. If you could see yourself! Quite a change from your entrance here this morning.

SILIA *(on the verge of tears)*: That seems unnatural to you? How should I feel?

LEONE: I wasn't making fun of you, Silia. I laughed because I've always enjoyed seeing you react so spontaneously, so openly to everything! Because you are so natural!

SILIA *(snapping at him)*: Not like you!

LEONE: No, you're absolutely right. And it's lucky for you I'm not!

SILIA *(first angrily; then admiringly; finally supplicatingly)*: I don't understand you . . . I don't understand you . . . I don't understand you.

LEONE *(going to her, tenderly)*: You can't, my dear. You never will. But it's better this way, believe me. *(A pause, then in a low voice:)* I'm the one who understands.

SILIA *(glancing at him, frightened)*: What do you understand?

LEONE *(calmly)*: What it is you want.

SILIA: Then what do I want? Tell me.

LEONE: You know . . . and you don't know what you desire from life.

SILIA: Oh, God, Leone, I'm afraid I'm going mad!

LEONE: Of course you aren't.

SILIA: Yes, I am. I must have been mad to cause all this trouble.

LEONE: Don't be frightened. I'm here.

SILIA: But what will you do?

LEONE: What I've always done, from the day you taught me I had only one other choice.

SILIA: I taught you that?

LEONE: Yes, you.

SILIA: What other choice?

LEONE *(a pause, then softly)*: To kill you. *(Another pause.)* Don't you think that more than once you gave me every reason to? Oh, yes, you know I'm right, Silia. But this impulse sprang fully armed from the feeling I had for you—a feeling first of love, then of hatred! To save you I had to disarm these two powerful emotions, to get rid of them. And I did get rid of them, so I wouldn't have to kill you . . . So that you could live, not as you would like to—because you haven't any idea what it is you want from life—but the only way you can, the way you must, since you can never do as I do.

SILIA *(imploringly)*: What *do* you do, Leone?

LEONE *(after a long pause, then vaguely and sadly)*: I . . . abstract myself. *(Another pause.)* Do you think I have no feelings, no emotions? Of course I do. But I never let them get away from me. I seize them, I dominate them and I nail them up. Have you ever seen a trainer at work in a cage full of wild beasts? That's what I am, Silia: a lion tamer. But even as I play this part, I can stand aside and laugh at myself in my chosen role. And I confess that sometimes I have a terrible temptation to give in, to let myself be torn apart by one of these savage beasts. Even as I stand here now and look at you, so gentle and so sad . . . But I can't! I won't! Because, you see, it's all a game. And to give in is to put an end to it, to deprive you forever of the one pleasure life affords. No . . . Please go now, Silia . . .

SILIA *(hesitant, trembling, as if offering herself)*: Can't I . . . don't you . . . want me . . . to stay?

LEONE: You?

SILIA: Or do you want me to come back tonight, when they've all gone?

LEONE: No. No, my dear. All my strength, all—

SILIA: Just to be near you, Leone. To . . . to help you.

LEONE: Don't worry. Sleep is all the help I need, my dear, and I always sleep soundly. Tonight and every night. A deep and dreamless sleep.

SILIA *(with deeply-felt bitterness)*: You see? This is why it's so hopeless! You won't believe me, I suppose, when I tell you that in bed my real love has always been the sleep that rescued me by allowing me to dream.

LEONE: To dream? Yes, I believe you. I believe you.

SILIA: But it never happens any more! I never sleep! And certainly not tonight! *(Abruptly breaking off.)* Enough! I'll be here tomorrow morning.

LEONE: No! No, I don't want you to come, you know! I don't want you!

SILIA: You don't want me to come? You're joking!

LEONE: I forbid you to! I tell you, I don't want you!

SILIA: You can't stop me, Leone! I'll be here!

LEONE: All right, then . . . then do as you like.

(Filippo enters with the luncheon tray.)

FILIPPO: Oh! It's time!

SILIA *(dramatically)*: Till tomorrow then!

LEONE *(quietly)*: Yes, until tomorrow . . .

(Silia exits. Leone stands immobile, lost in thought, then slowly turns and walks toward the table.)

CURTAIN

ACT III

Leone's house at dawn the following morning.

The curtain rises on an empty, dimly-lit stage. The door-bell rings and Filippo enters. Grumbling to himself, he goes to answer it.

FILIPPO: Who the devil can that be, at this hour? Oh, we're off to a fine start! *(He exits and returns a moment later, followed by Dr. Spiga, who is elaborately attired in a swallow-tailed coat and a top hat. He also carries two large, heavy suitcases.)*

SPIGA: What? Still asleep?

FILIPPO: Yes. Keep your voice down.

SPIGA: Oh. I'm sorry . . . By God, still asleep! And I didn't get a wink all night!

FILIPPO: Worried? About him? *(He indicates Leone's door.)*

SPIGA: Of course. And with trying to remember to bring everything.

FILIPPO *(indicating the suitcases)*: What's in there?

SPIGA: Everything I'll need. More than everything, I hope. *(Approaching the dining table, which is covered by a tablecloth.)* All right, let's clear this off now.

FILIPPO: What for?

SPIGA: I brought one of my own. *(He opens one of his bags and produces a white surgical sheet.)*

FILIPPO: What are you going to do with that?

SPIGA: Lay out my things, of course.

FILIPPO: Certainly not! Don't you dare touch that table! Can't you see I'm about to set it for breakfast?

SPIGA: Breakfast? This is no time to think about breakfast! Get out of my way!

FILIPPO: I said don't touch it!

SPIGA *(turning toward the writing desk)*: Then clear this one off!

FILIPPO: Are you joking? Don't you understand that these two tables—talk to us?

SPIGA: As if I didn't know! Don't start quoting him to *me! (Imitating Leone.)* Two symbols: the writing desk and the dining table, my books and my cooking utensils, the clear head and the full stomach—I've heard it all! What you don't seem to realize is that none of this clever nonsense is going to do him much good this morning!

FILIPPO: Is that so? I suppose you've already ordered his coffin? You certainly look like an undertaker!

SPIGA: A monster! My God, what an unfeeling monster! For your information, I was told to dress this way. The things I have to put up with! And after the night I've passed! If you only knew—

FILIPPO: Keep your voice down!

SPIGA *(softly)*: I'm not going to stand here and argue with you! Hurry up! Let's at least clear off the coffee table. I have no time to lose.

FILIPPO: That's easy. No sooner said . . . *(he removes an ash tray and a vase of flowers)* . . . than done! There you are.

SPIGA *(spreading his sheet over the table)*: Oh, at last! *(Now, while Spiga goes to work emptying the suitcases of his gleaming, horrible surgical instruments and laying them out on the sheet, Filippo bustles about, in and out of the kitchen, setting the dining table.)* Now let's see . . . I think I have everything . . . scalpels . . . clamps . . . forceps . . . scissors . . . bone saws . . . compressors . . .

FILIPPO: What do you need that butcher shop for?

SPIGA: What do I need it for? There's going to be some

fighting here, haven't you heard? A bullet in the wrong place and we may even have to amputate, God save us! He could easily lose a leg . . . an arm . . .

FILIPPO: Wonderful! And where's your supply of artificial limbs?

SPIGA: It isn't as funny as you think. We have to be prepared for anything. To extract the bullet I brought along all these little tools: a probe . . . tweezers . . . my new extractor. Look, it's an English model. Exquisite, isn't it? Oh, but where are my needles? *(He searches in one of the bags.)* Ah, here they are! A stitch in time. . . Well, I guess that's everything. *(Looking at his watch.)* It's six twenty-five, you know. The seconds will be here any minute.

FILIPPO: What do I care?

SPIGA: I didn't mean you. I know you don't care. I meant him. He's not even awake yet.

FILIPPO: It's too early.

SPIGA: This is hardly the day to hold him to his regular schedule. He has an appointment at seven o'clock!

FILIPPO: Then let him wake himself up and get dressed. He may even be up, for all I know.

SPIGA: You could go and take a look!

FILIPPO: I will not! You don't catch me in there at this hour! My job is to be his clock on normal days and I will not set myself ahead or behind by so much as a minute. Reveille at seven-thirty!

SPIGA: Don't you realize that today he might be dead by seven-thirty?

FILIPPO: And at eight I bring him his breakfast.

(The doorbell rings.)

SPIGA: There, you see? They're here!

(Filippo goes to open the door and returns, followed by Guido and Barelli.)

GUIDO *(entering)*: Ah, my dear Doctor. . . .

BARELLI: Good morning, Doctor.

SPIGA: Good morning, good morning.

GUIDO: Are we all ready?

SPIGA: I am, anyway. At least, as ready as I can be.

BARELLI *(laughing at the sight of Spiga's surgical layout)*: Look, look, Guido! He really is prepared! You set a full table, Doctor.

GUIDO *(irritated)*: Good God, Barelli! That's nothing to laugh about! *(To Spiga:)* Has *he* seen it?

SPIGA: Who? Excuse me, but . . . *quod abundat non vitiat.* That's Latin for—

GUIDO: Never mind that now. I was asking whether Leone has seen this lovely sight. *(To Barelli:)* You understand, Barelli, he needs absolute calm and if he sees—

SPIGA: Oh, he hasn't seen anything yet. No, indeed.

GUIDO: Where is he?

SPIGA: Well, it seems he isn't up yet.

BARELLI: What?

GUIDO: Not up yet?

SPIGA: Apparently not. At least, I haven't seen him.

GUIDO: Well, my God, let's not waste any time! It comes off in fifteen minutes. He must be up! *(To Filippo:)* Go and tell him right away that we're here!

BARELLI: The man's magnificent!

GUIDO *(to Filippo, who has been standing there, motionless, frowning)*: Move! Do you hear me?

FILIPPO: At seven-thirty.

GUIDO: Oh, go to hell! I'll call him myself. *(He runs toward the bedroom door.)*

SPIGA: He must be up by now.

BARELLI: He's incredible, I tell you!

GUIDO *(banging loudly on the door and listening for sounds of movement from within)*: What's he doing? Sleeping? *(Banging more loudly and calling.)* Leone! Leone! *(He listens, then turns to the others.)* It's true! He's still asleep! Would you believe it? Still asleep! *(Banging on the door and trying the doorknob.)* Leone! Leone!

BARELLI: Magnificent! Truly magnificent!

GUIDO: What is this? He locks himself in?

FILIPPO: With a double bolt. He doesn't want to be surprised.

BARELLI: And he's such a sound sleeper?

FILIPPO: The soundest. It takes me at least two minutes, every morning, to wake him up.

GUIDO: By God, I'll break the door in if I have to! Leone! Leone! . . . Ah, there he is. . . He's awake now. . . Yes, believe it or not, he's just waking up! *(Shouting through the keyhole.)* Leone! Get dressed! Quickly! There isn't a moment to lose! We're waiting for you. Hurry up, for God's sake! It's almost seven o'clock.

BARELLI: My friends, he's unbelievable. If I hadn't seen it with my own eyes . . .

SPIGA: And what a sleeper!

FILIPPO: Every morning it's like hauling him up from the bottom of a well.

GUIDO: Any danger he'll fall back in? I'd better make sure. *(He turns back toward the door as Filippo exits into the kitchen.)*

BARELLI *(hearing the noise of the bolt being drawn)*: No, here he is. He's opening up.

SPIGA *(placing himself in front of the coffee table)*: I'll cut off the view from this side.

(The bedroom door now opens to reveal Leone, dressed in pajamas and slippers. He is still a bit sleepy, and supremely calm.)

LEONE: Good morning.

GUIDO: What? Still in your pajamas? Go and get dressed, for God's sake! You haven't a moment to lose.

LEONE: I haven't? What's the hurry?

GUIDO: What do you mean, what's the hurry?

BARELLI: You have a duel to fight, remember?

LEONE: I have?

SPIGA: He's still asleep.

GUIDO: Yes, the duel! The duel! At seven o'clock!

BARELLI: It's ten of seven now!

LEONE: I understand. I can hear you. And I want you to know I'm wide-awake.

GUIDO *(absolutely flabbergasted)*: Well?

BARELLI: What does this mean, Leone?

LEONE *(very calmly)*: That's what I was going to ask you.

SPIGA *(under his breath)*: The strain has been too much for him, poor fellow.

LEONE: No, my dear Doctor, I'm perfectly sane, thank you.

GUIDO: Leone, you have a duel to fight!

LEONE: I'm supposed to fight it, too?

BARELLI: What do you mean, too?

LEONE: No, no, my friends, you're mistaken.

BARELLI: You don't want to fight?

GUIDO: You wish to withdraw?

LEONE: I? Withdraw? You know perfectly well I never budge an inch from where I stand.

GUIDO: But we find you like this . . .

BARELLI: And you say–

LEONE: How do you find me? What am I supposed to say? All I have to tell you, Guido, is that you and my wife upset my whole day yesterday trying to force me to do what I immediately realized I had to do.

GUIDO: Well, then–

BARELLI: So you will fight!

LEONE: No. That part of it isn't up to me.

BARELLI: Then who is it up to?

LEONE: It's up to him. *(He indicates Guido.)*

BARELLI: Guido?

LEONE: Yes, Guido, Guido. Who else? *(He walks over to Guido, who has turned white, and looks deeply into his eyes.)* And you know it! (*Turning to Barelli.*) He knows it, all right! As the husband, I, of course, had to send the challenge. He couldn't very well be expected to do that, in his somewhat unofficial capacity. But as for fighting the duel itself, that's something else. Oh, as for the actual fighting, Barelli, no, thank you. *(To Guido, softly, almost affectionately toying with the lapel of Guido's coat and emphasizing each word:)* You know I'm right, don't you? You know it isn't up to me. I'm not going to fight the duel. You are.

(Guido wipes the cold sweat off his brow with trembling hands.)

BARELLI: But this is monstrous!

LEONE: Not at all, my friend. It's the most natural thing in the world, if you understand the rules of the game. We all have our parts to play in it—I have mine, he has his. From the pivot of my concept I will not move. You see, Barelli, I understand the game, and so does Miglioriti. You told me yourself that the marquis was very angry at Guido, not at me. That it's Guido he wants to fight, not me. Because everyone knows, and you better than anyone else, what they tried to do to me. *(To Guido:)* So you really did intend to lead me to the slaughter?

GUIDO *(protesting strongly)*: No! I didn't! I didn't!

LEONE: Go on! Between you and my wife here yesterday it was like a game of seesaw, with me sitting in the middle, watching the two of you go up and down, up and down. And all the time you thought you were toying with me, with my life. Well, you missed your shot; I was toying with you.

GUIDO: No, that isn't it! You were here yesterday when I protested . . . right from the start—

LEONE: Oh, yes, you protested warmly. You were the very soul of discretion.

GUIDO: What do you mean? What are you insinuating?

LEONE: Well, Guido, you *were* discreet and you *did* protest Silia's behavior, but not that completely, you must admit. At a certain point, for reasons I understand all too clearly, you changed your mind and suddenly became quite enthusiastic about making all the arrangements. Rash, in fact. And I'm sorry for you, because now you'll have to take the consequences.

GUIDO: You don't intend to fight?

LEONE: I have no reason to.

GUIDO: I see. Then it's up to me?

LEONE: Of course.

SPIGA *(to Leone)*: But you sent the challenge. How can he–

LEONE: Tell him, Barelli.

BARELLI: Well, under ordinary circumstances, if a principal withdraws or is unable to appear, then his second is expected to substitute for him.

LEONE: You see?

GUIDO: All right then. I will!

BARELLI: But these aren't ordinary circumstances! I–I won't permit this! I–

GUIDO: Wait a minute, Barelli. *(To Leone scornfully:)* Now what are you going to do?

LEONE: Have breakfast.

GUIDO: No, I mean . . . Don't you understand, Leone, that if I take your place–

LEONE: Not my place, Guido. Yours.

GUIDO: All right, have it your way: mine. But if I do that, you'll be the laughingstock of the whole town!

BARELLI: He's right. You'll be completely dishonored!
(Leone laughs heartily.)
You can laugh? Publicly disgraced and you can laugh?

LEONE: Certainly I can laugh. Don't you see how I live here? And where I live? Do you think I care what anyone thinks?

GUIDO: Come on, Barelli, we're wasting time. Let's go.

BARELLI: You really are going to fight?

GUIDO: You heard him. I have no choice.

BARELLI: Perhaps I could do something. I don't see why—

LEONE: He knows it's up to him, Barelli. Believe me. He knows.

BARELLI: You're being cynical.

LEONE: Not at all. When you can rid yourself of sentiment, Barelli, and apply the force of logic, then perhaps you'll understand.

GUIDO *(interrupting and seizing Barelli's arm)*: Come on, Barelli, there's no time to argue any more. Doctor, please follow us!

SPIGA: Coming, coming!

(At this point Silia enters. There is a brief silence, during which she stands hesitant and confused.)

GUIDO *(stepping forward to take her hand)*: Good-by, Silia. *(Then, turning to Leone.)* Good-by. *(He rushes out, followed at once by Barelli and Spiga.)*

SILIA: What does this mean?

LEONE: I told you, my dear, that it was useless for you to come. However, you insisted . . .

SILIA: But you . . . What are you doing here?

LEONE: I live here.

SILIA: But then . . . but he . . . Has the duel been called off?

LEONE: I don't think so. It's probably just getting under way.

SILIA: But how? If you're still here?

LEONE: Oh, yes, I'm still here. But Guido isn't. Didn't you see him make his exit?

SILIA: What? Oh, God! You mean . . . you mean he went in your place? He went to fight for you?

LEONE: Not for me, my dear. For you!

SILIA: For me? Oh, God! For me, you said? Oh! And you made him do it? You're responsible for this?

LEONE *(advancing on her with all the scorn and majesty of a judge)*: I'm responsible? You have the impudence to suggest that I'm responsible for all this?

SILIA: You took advantage of us!

LEONE *(dramatically)*: No! I punished you!

SILIA *(scathingly)*: And covered yourself with shame!

LEONE *(seizing her by the arm and flinging her away from him)*: *You* are my only shame!

SILIA: *(peering wildly around the room)*: Oh, God! And meanwhile . . . Oh, God, how awful! It's horrible! Where are they? In the garden? Fighting under those conditions? The ones Guido insisted on? Oh, it's just perfect, isn't it! And you—you backed him up! You told him he was right! Of course you would! You knew you wouldn't have to risk your neck! Oh, God, you're the devil himself! You're— Where are they, Leone? Where are they fighting? In the garden? *(She searches about for a window.)*

LEONE: Not that way. There aren't any windows in the back. You can either go around the front or climb up on the roof . . . Wonderful view from up there . . . This way, Silia.

(At this point Spiga enters precipitously. He is deathly pale and terribly upset. He hurls himself at the coffee table, scoops up the entire load of surgical instruments, and flings the sheet, like a sack, over his shoulder. Without uttering a word he starts back toward the door.)

SILIA: Ah, Doctor! Doctor! Please! Tell me! Tell me! What happened?

(Spiga does not answer. Silia screams. Hardly daring to

believe her own words.) Dead? *(Running after the doctor.)* Dead? Is he dead?

(Leone stands very still, absorbed in his gloomy thoughts. A long pause. Finally, Filippo enters with Leone's breakfast tray and puts it down on the dining table. Then, in the tragic silence, he calls to Leone in a muffled, hollow voice.)

FILIPPO: Oh!

(Leone barely turns his head. Filippo points uncertainly to the breakfast tray.) It's . . . it's time!

(As if he hadn't heard him, Leone does not move.)

CURTAIN

THE PLEASURE OF HONESTY

(Il piacere dell'onestà)

CHARACTERS

FIRST MAID
MAURIZIO SETTI
MADDALENA RENNI
FABIO COLLI
AGATA RENNI
ANGELO BALDOVINO
MARCHETTO FONGI
SECOND MAID
THE RECTOR
THE DIRECTORS OF THE BOARD (Four Men)
A NURSE

ACT I

The living room of the Renni household, in a provincial town of central Italy. Morning.

ACT II

The same room, in what has become the Baldovino household, about ten months later.

ACT III

The same, the following morning.

TIME: *The present.*

ACT I

An elegant living room in the Renni house. Exits lead to the front hall and Agata's bedroom. Another exit leads into a studio, not used in Act I. At curtain, the room is empty. Then a maid ushers in Maurizio Setti. He is thrity-eight years old, well dressed, casual, a good talker, worldly, with something of the adventurer about him.

MAID: This way, please. I'll tell them you're here.
(She exits into the bedroom.)
(After a few seconds Maddalena Renni enters. She is in her early fifties, chic, still beautiful, but resigned to her years. A devoted mother, she sees everything through her daughter's eyes. At the moment she is worried, anxious.)

MADDALENA: Setti, at last! Well?

MAURIZIO: He's here. We arrived together this morning.

MADDALENA: And . . . it's all arranged?

MAURIZIO: Yes.

MADDALENA: You explained everything clearly?

MAURIZIO: Everything, everything. Don't worry.

MADDALENA *(hesitantly)*: You're sure? I mean, he understands–

MAURIZIO: Oh, God, I suppose so. I–I just told him what the situation was, that's all.

MADDALENA *(bowing her head, bitterly)*: The situation . . . oh, yes.

MAURIZIO: I couldn't very well not tell him, Mrs. Renni.

MADDALENA: I know, I know, but–

MAURIZIO: And then it all depends on how you look at it. I mean, who the person was, the circumstances, the time and the place. All these things matter.

MADDALENA: Yes, you're right. That's it exactly.

MAURIZIO: And you can be very sure I made all that perfectly clear to him.

MADDALENA: What kind of people we are? Who my daughter is? And he accepted? No difficulties?

MAURIZIO: No difficulties. Stop worrying.

MADDALENA: Stop worrying? How can I help but worry? Tell me about him.

MAURIZIO: Well, he's a good-looking man. No Adonis, but very presentable, you'll see. Unaffected, with a certain dignity about him. And from a very good family.

MADDALENA: But what kind of person is he? I mean, his character?

MAURIZIO: A good man, I'm sure.

MADDALENA: Can he talk? Does he know what to say?

MAURIZIO: Oh, Mrs. Renni, the Baldovinos have always been splendid talkers!

MADDALENA: No, I mean, can he be trusted? You see, even one indiscretion, one word without that certain— *(Just above a whisper, hardly able to express herself.)*—that certain . . . Oh, dear, I don't know how to put it! *(She begins to cry.)*

MAURIZIO: You mustn't take it so hard, Mrs. Renni.

MADDALENA: My poor Agata would just die!

MAURIZIO: No, you can rest easy on that score, Mrs. Renni. He's a most tactful man. I guarantee it. Very reserved, absolutely correct—a real gentleman. And extremely sensitive. There's no reason to worry. I guarantee it.

MADDALENA: My dear Setti, you have no idea how awful this is! I feel so lost . . . so helpless . . . To find yourself suddenly faced with such a decision! It's one of those disasters—well, you know, as if you opened a door into your private life and every passing stranger could walk in and snoop around.

MAURIZIO: Well, that's life . . .

MADDALENA: And that poor daughter of mine! That gentle heart! If you could see her, if you could hear her! It's so dreadful!

MAURIZIO: I can imagine. Mrs. Renni, I've done all I could to–

MADDALENA *(interrupting, clasping his hand)*: I know! I know! And can't you see I have no secrets from you? Because you're like one of the family. More than a cousin–a brother to our dear Fabio.

MAURIZIO: Is Fabio here?

MADDALENA: Yes, he's in there, with her. We can't leave her alone yet. The minute she heard you were back, she ran for the window.

MAURIZIO: Oh, my God! Because of me?

MADDALENA: No. Because she knows why you went away and with whom you'd be returning.

MAURIZIO: But–but I thought–I thought . . .

MADDALENA: She's almost in hysterics. So worked up it frightens me.

MAURIZIO: But–I'm sorry, but wasn't it all agreed? Didn't she give her consent?

MADDALENA: Yes. Of course.

MAURIZIO *(astounded)*: And she's changed her mind?

MADDALENA: No, no. How could she? What else can she do? She has to go through with it. She simply has to.

MAURIZIO: You're right. She must realize that.

MADDALENA: Oh, Setti, this will kill her!

MAURIZIO: Now, Mrs. Renni, you mustn't–

MADDALENA: It will kill her! Even if she doesn't do something foolish! It's partly my fault, I know. I thought . . . I thought Fabio would be more careful . . .

(Maurizio shrugs helplessly.)

You shrug? Yes, you're right. What else can we do now but shrug, shut our eyes, and allow our shame to overwhelm us?

MAURIZIO: Now, Mrs. Renni, you mustn't feel that way. We're all of us doing our best—

MADDALENA *(hiding her face in her hands)*: No! Please don't talk like that! Please! It makes it worse! Believe me, Setti, I feel nothing but remorse for my weakness. That's all it was at first—just weakness.

MAURIZIO: I understand, Mrs. Renni.

MADDALENA: How can you understand? You're a man, Setti, and not even a father. How can you know what a mother feels when she sees her daughter growing older, beginning to lose the first flower of her youth? You no longer dare to be as strict as you think you ought to be, as your own honesty compels you to be. Ah, Setti, your own sense of honesty can become a mockery! When your daughter looks at you with eyes begging for understanding, for indulgence, what is a mother to say? I know the world . . . I've been in love . . . . And so you pretend not to notice, and your pretense and your silence make you equally responsible until you come . . . you come to this! But I did think, I did think Fabio would be more careful.

MAURIZIO: Well, it's not always easy, Mrs. Renni.

MADDALENA: I know. I know.

MAURIZIO: If he could have done anything—

MADDALENA: I know. I can see he's as upset as I am, poor man. And if he hadn't been really in love with her, do you think any of this could have happened?

MAURIZIO: Fabio is a fine man.

MADDALENA: And we knew he was unhappy, separated from that terrible wife of his. You see, the very thing that should have prevented all this from happening is what has got us into this mess! Tell me in all confidence,

Setti: if Fabio had been free, he would have married my daughter, wouldn't he?

MAURIZIO: Oh, undoubtedly.

MADDALENA: Don't lie to me. Please. You do believe that, don't you?

MAURIZIO: Mrs. Renni, can't you see for yourself how much he loves her? What a state he's in?

MADDALENA: It's true, then? It's really true? You don't know how comforting it is to hear you say that, at such a time!

MAURIZIO: My dear Mrs. Renni, you know I've never had anything but the highest respect, the most sincere and devoted affection for you and Miss Agata.

MADDALENA: Thank you, thank you.

MAURIZIO: You must believe that. Or I would never have involved myself in the matter at all.

MADDALENA: Thank you, Setti. Believe me, when a woman, a serious young woman, has waited so many years, so patiently, for a man worthy of her and has been unable to find one, when at last she does fall in love with a man and knows that this man has been wronged, embittered, unjustly hurt by another woman—believe me, it's impossible to resist the spontaneous impulse to show him that not all women are like his wife, that there are women who will return your love and not trample you under their feet.

MAURIZIO: Yes, that's it exactly! Trampled underfoot, poor Fabio. You're quite right, Mrs. Renni. He didn't deserve it.

MADDALENA: You say to yourself, "No, you can't. You mustn't." And for a while you keep silent, you smother your feelings, your anguish—

MAURIZIO: And then it happens . . .

MADDALENA: Yes, it happens. And always when you least expect it. It was a wonderful spring night. I was leaning out the window. Outside, the perfume of flowers, a sky full of stars. Inside, my anguish, my love for her. And everything in me cried out, "Why shouldn't she have all this, too, just once—all those flowers, all those stars!". . . . And so I stayed there, in the shadows, knowing what would happen, all of us the helpless victims of an act of nature for which the next day society and our own consciences would condemn us. But at that moment, Setti, you're glad it's happening, you know in every fiber of your being that it *has* to happen, and you feel a strange sense of satisfaction and pride, even though you know you'll pay for it tomorrow . . . That's the way it was, Setti . . . I know we were wrong, but what could we do? It would be so easy if afterward you could just disappear. But you can't. You have to go on living, and by all the rules you threw away in a single rash moment.

MAURIZIO: Yes, I know. And that's exactly why we have to act calmly and sensibly now. You realize that you've all given in far too much to your feelings.

MADDALENA: You're right, of course.

MAURIZIO: Well, now we have to put our feelings aside and listen to the voice of reason, don't we?

MADDALENA: Yes, yes.

MAURIZIO: The fact is there's no time to lose. So—ah, here's Fabio!

(Fabio enters. He is forty-three, a likable and honorable man, but with enough weakness in his make-up to suggest he might be one of those men who are inevitably unlucky in love. He is terribly upset and rushes to Maddalena.)

FABIO: Please! Go in there! Don't leave her alone!

MADDALENA: Yes, of course. But it seems—

FABIO: Please! Quickly!

MADDALENA: Yes, yes! *(To Maurizio:)* Excuse me. *(She exits into the bedroom.)*

MAURIZIO: Fabio! You, too?

FABIO: Please, Maurizio, don't say it! You think you found a solution? I'll tell you what you did! You painted a corpse!

MAURIZIO: I what?

FABIO: All you've done is make it look possible!

MAURIZIO: But it was your idea! Now, listen–I'm not in this because I enjoy it!

FABIO: I'm suffering, I'm suffering, Maurizio! That poor creature in there! It's hell! And this solution of yours doesn't make it any easier. In fact, it makes it worse, because I know it's the only way out, understand? But it's an external solution: all it can do is save appearances, nothing else.

MAURIZIO: Doesn't that matter any more? Four days ago that's all you could think about. And now that we have the chance–

FABIO: I can't go through with it! Does that seem so wrong?

MAURIZIO: Yes! Because that way you lose everything! Appearances don't matter? Of course they do, and you know it! You can't be objective about it, but I can. And I'm going to force you to go through with it, to paint the corpse, as you put it . . . He's here. We arrived together. Now, if we have to move quickly–

FABIO: Yes, all right. Tell me, tell me. Yes, I know it's the only way. You warned him I wouldn't turn over a penny of the estate?

MAURIZIO: Yes.

FABIO: And he accepted?

MAURIZIO: I told you, he's here with me. All he asks, and I don't think it's unreasonable, is the liquidation of his past. And only because he wants to be able to fulfill all the obligations he assumes toward you—and the conditions you imposed. He has a few debts.

FABIO: How many? A lot? I can just imagine!

MAURIZIO: No, only a few. My God, Fabio, what did you expect? He has a few debts. But he wanted me to tell you—he was very insistent on this point—that his debts are few only because he ran out of credit, not because of any reluctance on his part to make them.

FABIO: Oh, fine!

MAURIZIO: That's honest, anyway. You understand, if he still had any credit he wouldn't have to—

FABIO: All right, all right! That's enough! Now, tell me exactly what you said to him. What's he like? Shabby? A wreck?

MAURIZIO: He's a little run-down since the last time I saw him. But that's easily remedied. In fact, he looks better already. You know, with him it's largely a question of morale. The bad things he's been forced to do—

FABIO: Does he gamble? Swindle? Steal? What does he do?

MAURIZIO: He used to gamble. They won't let him any more. I found him so bitter it shocked me. We spent the whole night walking along the road near his home. Have you ever been in that part of the country?

FABIO: No.

MAURIZIO: I tell you, it was a fantastic night. We walked up and down that road, among the winking lights of great swarms of fireflies, and beside me all the time that man talking steadily, with the most terrifying frankness. And like the fireflies, his words would flash in the air around you, suddenly illuminating the very darkest corners of your soul. I had the feeling after a while that we were no longer on the earth but in some strange dreamland, a dark, mysterious country where he ruled, where the most bizarre, the most unbelievable things could happen and seem both natural and usual. He guessed what I was thinking—he notices everything—he smiled and talked to me about Descartes.

FABIO: Who?

MAURIZIO: Descartes, the philosopher. Well, you'll see—he's an extremely well-educated man, especially in philosophy. He told me that Descartes—

FABIO: For God's sake, Maurizio, what the hell do I care about Descartes?

MAURIZIO: Let me finish! You will care, you'll see. He told me that Descartes, in examining our sense of reality, had one of the most terrifying thoughts any human being has ever had: that if our dreams had any regularity, we would no longer be able to distinguish between sleeping and waking! Have you ever noticed how disturbing it is to have the same dream more than once? You begin to think you're dealing with something tangible, something real. Because our whole knowledge of the world hangs on this very slender thread: the re-gu-la-ri-ty of our experiences. We who live regular lives, by certain set rules, cannot imagine what can seem real or unreal to a man who lives outside any such pattern, like Baldovino. That's why I eventually found it so easy to make our proposition to him. He was talking about some plans of his that seemed so impossible to me, outrageous and impractical, that our scheme suddenly seemed ridiculously simple, so obvious and sensible that anyone would have agreed to it. That surprises you? Well, I wasn't even the one to bring up the money question. He immediately said he didn't want a cent for himself and wouldn't even discuss the matter. And you know why?

FABIO: Why?

MAURIZIO: Because he maintains it's much easier to be a

hero than a gentleman. Anyone can be heroic from time to time, but a gentleman is something you have to be all the time. Which isn't easy.

FABIO: Ah! *(Disturbed, irritated, gloomy, he begins to pace up and down.)* So . . . so he's apparently a man of some talent, eh?

MAURIZIO: Oh, a great deal of talent. Perhaps even a genius.

FABIO: Obviously he's never known how to use this talent.

MAURIZIO: Never. Even when he was a boy. We were classmates in school, as I told you. With his ability he could have done anything. But he studied only what he liked, all the most useless things. And he says that a practical education is the enemy of wisdom because you have to learn so many things which, if you want to be really wise, you ought to do without. He had an expensive upbringing: all the tastes, habits, ambitions, even vices of his class. Then things went badly, his father went bankrupt and—well, it's no wonder . . .

FABIO *(resuming his pacing)*: And . . . and you say he's a handsome man?

MAURIZIO: Yes, very presentable. Why? *(He laughs.)* Admit it: now you're afraid I made too good a choice!

FABIO: Go on! I just—I just don't see where all this fits in, that's all. Talent, education—

MAURIZIO: Philosophy. Not entirely inappropriate in this case.

FABIO: Damn it, Maurizio, this is no time for jokes! I'm going out of my mind! I would have preferred someone else, that's all. A modest, unassuming, more respectable type—

MAURIZIO: —who wouldn't fool anyone! Come on, Fabio! You have to remember what kind of house this is! Do you think anyone would believe Agata would want to marry some homely, middle-aged nonentity? We had to find somebody more worthwhile, someone people could respect and believe in, so at least no one would wonder how Miss Renni could bring herself to marry an ugly, inferior man. And I have every reason to think–

FABIO: What?

MAURIZIO:–that she'll accept him. Not only that, but she'll thank me a little more warmly than you.

FABIO: Oh, yes! She'll pour out her gratitude! If you could hear what's going on in there! Did you tell him everything has to be done as soon as possible?

MAURIZIO: Of course. You'll see, he'll be a member of the family in no time.

FABIO: Now what do you mean by that?

MAURIZIO: Oh, God! I mean, well, you know . . .

(The maid runs in.)

MAID: Mr. Colli, you're wanted in here!

FABIO: I can't now! I have to go with my cousin. *(To Maurizio:)* I must see him–speak to him. *(To the maid:)* Tell Mrs. Renni I can't come now.

MAID: Yes, sir. *(She exits.)*

MAURIZIO: The hotel is just down the block.

FABIO: I'm going mad! Mad! Between her in there, crying her eyes out, and you out here–

MAURIZIO: Listen, Fabio, we made no definite commitments. And if you don't want to go through with this–

FABIO: I want to see him first, talk to him.

MAURIZIO: Well, let's go then.

MADDALENA *(entering, very upset)*: Fabio! Fabio, come in here! Don't leave her alone now! Please!

FABIO: Oh, God!

MADDALENA: She's in hysterics! Please come!

FABIO: But I have to–

MAURIZIO: No. Go to her, Fabio.

MADDALENA: Yes! Please!

MAURIZIO: Shall I bring him here? We're under no obligation. You can talk to him here. Perhaps that's the best way. For Miss Agata, too.

FABIO: Yes, yes. Go get him. But no commitments, remember! We'll talk first! *(He exits into the bedroom.)*

MAURIZIO *(calling after him)*: In a few minutes! We'll be right back! *(He exits out the back.)*

MADDALENA *(following him to the door)*: You're bringing him here?

(Agata and Fabio rush in from the bedroom. Agata, though beautiful, has a hard, suffering look, the result of her difficult situation. Desperate now, rebellious, dishevelled, she nevertheless gives the impression of a woman of character, a person who, once she knows what she must do, will avoid subterfuge and follow the dictates of her conscience.)

AGATA *(freeing herself from Fabio)*: Let me alone! No! Let me alone! Let me go! I've got to go!

MADDALENA: Darling, where? Where do you want to go?

AGATA: I don't know! Away from here!

FABIO: Agata! Agata, please!

MADDALENA: You don't know what you're saying!

AGATA: Let me alone! I'll go mad, I'll die! There's no way out for me! I can't stand it! *(She collapses into a chair.)*

MADDALENA: Wait till Fabio sees him at least! Talks to him! And you see him, too.

AGATA: No! Me? No! Don't you understand how horrible this is? Don't you see it's monstrous, what you want me to do?

MADDALENA: But, darling—but you said yourself there was no—

AGATA: No! I won't do it! I won't do it!

FABIO *(with desperate resolve)*: All right, then! If you don't want to go through with it, we won't! You're right:

it is monstrous! I couldn't agree more! But are you brave enough to face the situation with me?

MADDALENA: What are you talking about, Fabio? You're a man and you can ignore the scandal! But what about us? Two women alone in a town of this size! We'll be overwhelmed by the disgrace! It's entirely a question of choosing the lesser of two evils: a public scandal or—

AGATA:—or a private one! Mine alone! I'm the one who'll have to live with this man! To see him every day! A man who must be a scoundrel, a swine, to lend himself to such a scheme! *(She leaps to her feet and again tries to escape.)* No, no, I can't do it! I can't see him! Let me go! Let me go!

MADDALENA: But where? And what will you do? Face the scandal? If that's what you want, I'll . . . I'll . . .

AGATA *(throwing herself into her mother's arms, sobbing helplessly)*: No . . . for your sake, Mother . . . no . . . no . . . for you . . .

MADDALENA: For my sake? Darling, what have I got to do with it? You mustn't worry about me. There's no way we can spare each other the pain of all this. Nor can we run away from it. We have to stay here and face it, all three of us, because we're all to blame.

AGATA: No, Mother . . . not you . . . not you . . .

MADDALENA: I most of all, my child. And I'm suffering even more than you.

AGATA: No, Mother! Because I feel for you as well as for myself!

MADDALENA: And I only for you, and so it's worse for me. I can't share my pain, because I live only in you, my child. Now be calm—wait—we have to see—

AGATA: It's horrible! Horrible!

MADDALENA: I know. But let's talk to him first.

AGATA: I can't! Mother, I can't!

MADDALENA: But we're right here with you. There's no

trickery involved. We aren't hiding anything. We'll be right here all the time, both of us, Fabio and I–right beside you.

AGATA: But he'll come and live here, don't you see? Live here with us, Fabio! A man who knows what we're hiding from the world!

FABIO: And it will be in his own best interests to help us hide it, for his own sake, and he'll stick to the agreement. If he won't, then so much the better for us. The minute he says he won't go along with it any more I'll find a way to get rid of him. In any case, we won't need him any longer.

MADDALENA: You see? Of course! It doesn't have to go on forever. Just for a little while.

FABIO: A few months, a year at most. Why should it be permanent?

AGATA: No, no! We'll never get rid of him!

MADDALENA: Let's meet him first. Setti assured me–

FABIO: We'll find a way, Agata! We'll find a way!

MADDALENA: He's an intelligent man, and–

(The doorbell rings. A pause.)

That must be him.

AGATA: Let's go, let's go. Mother! Oh, God! *(She drags her mother toward the bedroom.)*

MADDALENA: Of course. Fabio will talk to him. We'll go in there, the two of us.

FABIO: Don't worry, darling.

(Maddalena and Agata exit.)

MAID *(appearing in the entrance)*: Mr. Setti and another gentleman.

FABIO: Tell them to come in.

(The maid exits and Maurizio appears, followed by Angelo Baldovino. He is about forty, with a serious, intelligent face. His hair is thinning and uncombed; he has a short reddish beard, a penetrating glance, and

speaks slowly in a deep voice. He dresses conservatively, a bit shabbily, and wears a pince-nez, which he almost always carries in his hand and uses to emphasize his words. He seems abstracted: his appearance, his way of talking, of smiling, indicate a man nurturing in himself a host of bitter memories from which he has evolved a curious personal philosophy full of irony and pity.)

MAURIZIO *(entering)*: Well, here we are. Fabio, my friend Angelo Baldovino.

(Fabio bows.)

(To Angelo:) Fabio Colli, my cousin.

(Angelo bows.)

FABIO: Please sit down.

MAURIZIO: You have things to discuss, so . . . so I'll leave you now. *(To Angelo, shaking his hand:)* We'll see each other later, back at the hotel, all right? Good-by, Fabio.

FABIO: Good-by.

(Maurizio exits.)

ANGELO *(sitting down, his pince-nez on the end of his nose, his head tilted back)*: I must begin by asking you a favor.

FABIO: Go ahead, go ahead.

ANGELO: Mr. Colli, you must be frank with me.

FABIO: Of course. I ask for nothing better.

ANGELO: Thank you. However, I'm not sure you understand what I mean by this word "frank."

FABIO: Well . . . I don't know . . . open . . . sincere.

(With one upraised finger Angelo indicates the negative.) What then?

ANGELO: It's not enough. You see, Mr. Colli, inevitably we construct ourselves.

FABIO: We what?

ANGELO: Let me explain. I enter this house and immediately I become what I have to become, what I can become: I construct myself. That is, I present myself to you in a form suitable to the relationship I wish to achieve with you. And, of course, you do the same with me. But behind these fabrications we present to each other are hidden our most secret thoughts, our most intimate feelings, all that we really are quite apart from the relationship we want to establish with each other. Have I made myself clear?

FABIO: Yes, yes, very clear. Perfectly clear. My cousin told me you were very intelligent.

ANGELO: And now you probably think I'm only trying to prove how brilliant I am.

FABIO: No, no . . . I only meant . . . I agree, I agree with what you said, that's all.

ANGELO: So I'll begin by speaking frankly. For some time, Mr. Colli, I've been disgusted by the wretched subterfuge I've had to resort to in my relationship with my equals, if you don't mind my including you in this category.

FABIO: Not at all, not at all.

ANGELO: I look at myself—I'm always looking at myself, Mr. Colli—and I say to myself, "Look at what you're doing now! How disgusting, how revolting!"

FABIO *(disconcerted, embarrassed)*: No . . . really! Why?

ANGELO: I'm sorry, because it's true. So then you might wonder why I do such things? And the answer is: because I can't help myself. To want to be one thing or another is easy, Mr. Colli. The whole problem lies in succeeding. We're not alone, you see. We ride through life on the beast within us. Beat the animal, but you can't make it think. Try to persuade a jackass not to rush to the edge of a precipice—beat it, whip it, kick it—it can't help going there. And afterward it looks at you reproachfully. Can you help feeling sorry for it? And I mean pity, not forgiveness. To forgive a jackass you'd have to be a bit of a jackass yourself. But to feel sorry for it, that's something else. Don't you think so?

FABIO: Oh, of course, of course. So now can we talk about us?

ANGELO: That's exactly what we're doing, Mr. Colli. I told you all this to make you realize that, feeling as I do about the situation, I must insist on maintaining my self-respect. To pretend would be horrible, disgusting, unbearable. The truth!

FABIO: Yes, exactly. Quite right. Now let's see if we understand each other . . .

ANGELO: I'll just ask you a few questions.

FABIO: What?

ANGELO: Just a few questions, if you don't mind.

FABIO: Oh, certainly. Go ahead.

ANGELO: Here we are. *(He takes a little black notebook from his pocket and leafs through it.)* The basic facts. Since we're going to be open with each other . . . You, sir, are the young woman's lover–

FABIO *(interrupting quickly)*: Now just a minute! I don't think that's nece–

ANGELO *(smiling calmly)*: You see? You won't even answer the very first question.

FABIO: Of course not! Because–because–

ANGELO *(quickly, severely)*: Because it isn't true? You mean you aren't her lover? Well, then–*(rising)*–you must excuse me. I told you I had my self-respect. I could not lend myself to a sad and humiliating comedy.

FABIO: What do you mean? This way we'll only . . . I mean, there's no need to–

ANGELO: You're wrong. I can only maintain my self-respect, for whatever it's worth, if you speak to me as you would to your own conscience. Either that, Mr. Colli, or there's nothing to be done. I will not take part in clumsy fictionalizing. The truth! Will you answer the question?

FABIO: All right . . . Yes, I am. But for God's sake put away that notebook! You're alluding to Miss Agata Renni?

ANGELO *(still looking through his notes. A pause)*: Agata Renni. Yes. She's twenty-seven years old?

FABIO: Twenty-six.

ANGELO *(checking his figures)*: Her birthday is in September, we're in May. So that makes her nearer twenty-seven. And—*(the notebook again)*—there's a mother?

FABIO: Now really!

ANGELO: I'm only being conscientious; nothing else, believe me. I intend to be conscientious in everything, Mr. Colli.

FABIO: Well, yes, Miss Renni has a mother.

ANGELO: How old, please?

FABIO: Oh, I don't know. Fifty-one, fifty-two.

ANGELO: That's all? You see, it would be better if there weren't a mother involved. The mother, Mr. Colli, is an enormous fabrication. But I knew there was a mother. So let's be generous and say fifty-three. You, Mr. Colli, must be about my age, more or less. I look older, I know. I'm forty-one.

FABIO: Oh, I'm older then. I'm forty-three.

ANGELO: My congratulations. You look much younger. Who knows? Maybe after a while I also . . . well . . . forty-three, yes. Now, if you'll excuse me, I must touch on another very delicate matter.

FABIO: My wife?

ANGELO: You're separated. No fault of yours, I know: you've been a perfect gentleman. But the world is not for the gentle, Mr. Colli. So the fault is mainly your wife's. And here you found a refuge. But life is little more than a loan shark: it exacts a very high rate of interest for the few pleasures it concedes.

FABIO: How true!

ANGELO: Who should know that better than I? And now,

Mr. Colli, it's your turn to pay. You find yourself threatened by the usurer and I am called in to settle your debt. You can't imagine how happy it makes me to be able to revenge myself like this on a society that has already cut off my own credit. To impose myself on life! To be able to say, "All right! This man took from life what he had no right to take and now I'll pay what he owes, because if I didn't a concept of honesty would disappear, the honor of an entire family would be compromised!" Mr. Colli, it's a great satisfaction to me! A revenge on life! That's the only reason I'm doing it. Do you doubt that? You have every right to because I'm like— May I strike a parallel?

FABIO: Of course, of course.

ANGELO: I'm like a man who wants to spend gold in a country where the money is made of paper. Everyone mistrusts such a man at first, it's only natural. You're tempted now to turn me down, aren't you? But it's real gold, Mr. Colli. I've never been able to spend it because I have it in my soul and not in my pockets. Otherwise . . .

FABIO: Well, that's splendid of you! Truly splendid! I couldn't ask for anything better, Mr. Baldovino. Honesty! Good will!

ANGELO: I have my own family traditions, too . . . Do you know what it means to be dishonest? The sacrifice of my self-respect, endless bitterness, remorse, disgust . . . Why shouldn't I want to be honest with you? You invite me to a double wedding in this house: not only do I marry the woman, but I espouse the concept of honesty.

FABIO: Yes, exactly. And it's enough. That's all I ask.

ANGELO: All? You think it's enough? What about the consequences?

FABIO: The consequences? I don't understand.

ANGELO: Oh, I see that you . . . Well, I realize how anxious you are to extricate yourself from a painful situation.

Which is probably why you treat the matter so lightly.

FABIO: Treat it lightly? No, no. On the contrary.

ANGELO: Let me explain. Mr. Colli, am I or am I not to be an honest man?

FABIO: But of course you are! It's the only condition I insist upon!

ANGELO: Excellent. In my feelings, my desires, in all my acts I am to be entirely honest. I feel this. I want it. And I intend to prove it to you. Well?

FABIO: Well what? I told you, that's all I ask of you.

ANGELO: But the consequences, my dear Colli, the consequences! Look: honesty, the honesty you want from me, what is it? Think about it. Nothing. An abstraction. A pure form. Let's call it an absolute. Now, if I'm to be honest, I must live the abstraction; I must lend substance to the form; I must embody the concept. And what will be the consequences? First of all, I shall have to be a tyrant.

FABIO: A tyrant?

ANGELO: Of course. Not because I want to be one, but because I am the form, I am the absolute. I shall insist that all appearances be respected, which, of course, will mean grave sacrifices from you, Miss Renni, and her mother. Your liberties will be restricted and you will have to observe all the abstract forms of social life. And —let's put all our cards on the table, Mr. Colli, so you'll grasp the full extent of my commitment—and you know what will happen? In all your dealings with me, face it, you will be judged, and not I. I have only one interest in the whole unpleasant business: the chance you give me of being an honest man.

FABIO: Yes. My dear sir . . . you understand . . . well, you said it yourself . . . I . . . I'm not really sure I follow you . . . I . . . oh, you're a marvelous talker, but . . . well, let's get back to earth again, for heavens' sake!

ANGELO: I? To earth? I can't.

FABIO: Why not? What do you mean?

ANGELO: I can't because of the very condition you impose on me. I have to deal in the abstract. The one thing I can't ever do is touch ground. Reality is not for me; it's for you. You can plant your feet in the earth. You talk and I'll listen. I'll be the intelligence that cannot forgive but pities.

FABIO *(indicating himself)*: The jackass?

ANGELO: If you like.

FABIO: I suppose you're right. Yes, you are right. Well, then—then I'll talk and you listen. That way maybe we'll reach an understanding.

ANGELO: We?

FABIO: Of course. Who else?

ANGELO: No, Mr. Colli, you have to reach an understanding with yourself. I know what I have to do. I told you all this—I don't usually talk so much—because I want you to realize what you're doing.

FABIO: Me?

ANGELO: Yes, you. For me it's easy. What do I actually do? Nothing. I represent the form. The act—and an ugly one—was committed by you and I appear to make amends. I am to cover up the reality. But if I'm to succeed, in the interests of all concerned, you must respect me, and it won't be easy for you. You'll have to respect not me, but the form, the form I represent: the honest husband of a respectable woman. Don't you want to respect it?

FABIO: Of course I do!

ANGELO: And don't you understand that the more honest you expect me to be, the more unyielding and tyrannous will be the form? That's why I warned you to beware of the consequences. Not for my sake, but for yours. You see, I have a philosophy to lean on. And to justify my behavior, under such conditions, all I have to do is remind myself that the woman I'm marrying is to become a mother.

FABIO: Yes. Exactly. Very true.

ANGELO: And in my relationship with her I shall always bear in mind the baby that will be born. I shall have a function to fulfill—a noble, worthy function, all bound up in the innocence of the child. Is that all right?

FABIO: Oh, fine! Fine!

ANGELO: For me, but not for you. Mr. Colli, the more you approve, the more trouble you pile up for yourself.

FABIO: How? Why? I don't see all these difficulties.

ANGELO: It's my duty to make you see them. You're a gentleman. The circumstances of life have forced you to behave dishonestly. But you can't do without your honesty! So you come to me and require me to take your place: I am to become the honest husband of a woman who can never be your wife, the honest father of a child you can never acknowledge. Am I right?

FABIO: Yes. Yes, it's true.

ANGELO: But if the woman is yours, not mine; if the child is yours, not mine—don't you understand that my honesty isn't enough? You will have to be honest with me. There's no other way. If I'm to be honest, we're all going to be honest. There's no other way.

FABIO: What? I don't understand. Just a minute. You're saying—

ANGELO: Ah! Now, at last, you feel the earth tremble under your feet!

FABIO: No, but . . . I mean . . . if things are going to be different—

ANGELO: Of course they are. You're going to make them different. These appearances you wish to save, Mr. Colli, are for all of us. You want to save them and I am here to help you. You also want to be an honest man. Think it over. It isn't going to be easy.

FABIO: But you know what our situation is . . .

ANGELO: Precisely because I do know. I'm speaking against my own interests, but I can't help it. I advise you to think it over very carefully. *(A pause. Fabio rises and begins to pace up and down in consternation. Angelo also rises and waits.)*

FABIO *(still pacing)*: Of course . . . of course you know . . . if I . . .

ANGELO: Yes. Yes, you'd better think some more about what I've said. And it might not be a bad idea to discuss it with Miss Renni. *(Glancing toward the bedroom door.)* Though that may not be necessary since—

FABIO *(turning on him)*: Since what?

ANGELO *(calmly, sadly)*: Oh . . . why shouldn't she listen, after all? . . . I'll go now. You can let me know what you decide. I'll be at the hotel. *(He starts out, then turns back.)* In the meantime, Mr. Colli, you can count on my complete discretion.

FABIO: I do count on it.

ANGELO *(seriously, slowly)*: I have many wrongs on my own conscience, and here I don't think anyone is to blame, really. One of life's misfortunes . . . Whatever your decision, I want you to know that I'll always be secretly grateful to my old schoolmate for having thought me worthy to assume such an honest obligation. *(He bows.)* Mr. Colli . . .

CURTAIN

ACT II

About ten months later, the living room of what has become the Baldovino household. A few new pieces of furniture are in evidence. At curtain, Fabio and Marchetto

Fongi are on stage. Fongi is about fifty, an old fox, short, stooped, shrewd, and not devoid of humor. He is holding his hat and cane in one hand and has the other one on the knob of the open door into the studio. Fabio stands off to one side, as if anxious not to make his presence known.

FONGI *(speaking into the studio)*: Thank you, thank you, Baldovino. . . . Yes, of course. . . . I'll be delighted to come. Thank you. . . . I'll be back, I'll be back with the other members of the board in about half an hour. Until then . . .

(He closes the door and turns toward Fabio, who now tiptoes up to him and winks conspiratorially.)

FABIO *(softly, eagerly)*: Well? Do you really think it will work?

FONGI *(nodding first)*: He fell for it! He fell for it all right!

FABIO: I thought so. It's been nearly a week.

FONGI *(holding up and wiggling three fingers)*: Three million! Three million lire! What did I tell you? It couldn't miss! *(He takes Fabio by the arm and leads him toward the front door.)* What a comedy! Leave it to me! Leave it to me! We'll catch him red-handed!

(They exit.)

(The room remains empty for a moment, then the studio door opens and Angelo and Maurizio enter. Angelo has changed considerably: he is soberly well dressed, more at ease, well groomed, less obvious in his mannerisms.)

MAURIZIO *(looking around)*: You know, you've really done all right for yourself.

ANGELO *(abstractedly)*: I suppose so. *(Smiling faintly.)* Everything handled with perfect decorum. *(A pause.)* Well, now, what about you? Where have you been?

MAURIZIO: Oh, here and there. Pretty far off the beaten track, actually.

ANGELO: You?

MAURIZIO: You don't believe me?

ANGELO: Off the beaten track? By which you mean you haven't been to Capri or Paris or the Riviera. Where have you been?

MAURIZIO: The land of rubber and bananas.

ANGELO: Africa?

MAURIZIO: The Congo. In the heart of the jungle. Oh, yes. Real jungle.

ANGELO: Ah! See any animals?

MAURIZIO: A few pygmies, some half-civilized natives.

ANGELO: No, I mean big game: tigers, leopards.

MAURIZIO: Oh, a handful of exhausted lions. Nothing much . . . What a strange look in your eyes.

ANGELO *(smiling bitterly, he cups his hand and shows Maurizio his nails)*: You see what we've come to? And we don't cut our nails to disarm ourselves, Maurizio. On the contrary: just to make us look more civilized, so we can hold our own in a far more desperate struggle than the one our ancestors fought with nothing but their claws. That's why I've always envied wild animals. And you, you rascal, all over Africa without even looking at the animals?

MAURIZIO: Oh, never mind about that. Let's talk about you. How's it going?

ANGELO: What?

MAURIZIO: I mean, with your wife? This—this arrangement?

ANGELO: How should it go? Everything's fine.

MAURIZIO: And—and your relationship?

ANGELO *(a pause. He looks at his friend, then rises)*: What did you expect?

MAURIZIO *(cheerfully)*: You look well, you know.

ANGELO: I keep busy.

MAURIZIO: Ah, yes. I heard Fabio organized a new syndicate of investors.

ANGELO: Yes. To get me into trouble. It's doing very nicely.

MAURIZIO: And you're in charge of it?

ANGELO: That's why it's so successful.

MAURIZIO: Yes, yes, so I was told. I'd like to get into it myself, but . . . Well, they say you're terribly strict.

ANGELO: That's right. I don't steal . . . *(Going up to Maurizio and resting his hands on his friend's arms.)* You know what it's like? To have hundreds of thousands passing through your hands? To think of all that money as just so much paper? Not to feel the slightest need for it or interest?

MAURIZIO: Oh, it must be great fun for you—

ANGELO: Divine! And not one mistake, not one failure! I work, I work hard. And they all have to go along with me.

MAURIZIO: Yes . . . that's it . . .

ANGELO: They complain, don't they? Tell me. They scream? They bite their nails?

MAURIZIO: They say—they say you could be a little less—well, a little less meticulous, that's all.

ANGELO: I know. I stifle them. I stifle everybody. Whoever comes close to me. But you see, there's nothing else I can do. For the past ten months I haven't been a human being.

MAURIZIO: No? What are you?

ANGELO: I've told you: almost a god! If you could only understand, Maurizio! I exist only in what seems to be. I bury myself in numbers, in financial speculations, but only for others. Not one cent of it—and I want it that way—not one cent of it is mine! I live here, in this beautiful house, and I can hardly see or hear or touch anything. Sometimes I'm amazed at the sound of my own voice, the echo of my own footsteps through these rooms; to discover that I need a drink of water or feel the need to rest. I live—do you see?—deliciously, in the absolute of a pure abstract form!

MAURIZIO: You ought to feel a little compassion for us poor mortals.

ANGELO: I do, but I can't help myself. However, I warned him, I warned your cousin well ahead of time. And I'm living up to the agreement we made.

MAURIZIO: But you seem to be taking malicious pleasure in it all.

ANGELO: Not malicious, no. Suspended in the air, it's like lying on a cloud: the joy of the saints as depicted in the great frescoes of our churches.

MAURIZIO: Still, you understand, it can't go on like this.

ANGELO *(gloomily, after a pause)*: Oh, I know. It will end. Soon, perhaps. But they'd better be careful! We'll see how it goes! *(Looking into his eyes.)* I'm saying this for their own sake. Open your cousin's eyes. He's too anxious to get rid of me as soon as possible. That disturbs you? You know something?

MAURIZIO: No, nothing.

ANGELO: Come on, be honest. I'm sorry for them. It's only natural.

MAURIZIO: I assure you I don't know anything. I spoke to Mrs. Renni, but I haven't even seen Fabio yet.

ANGELO: Oh, I know. They both thought, her mother and your cousin, they both thought: "We'll get the girl married, a mere formality. Then, after a while, on some pretext or other, we'll get rid of him." That was the best they could hope for, wasn't it? But they had no *right* to hope for it! From the very beginning they've both been deplorably frivolous.

MAURIZIO: Is that what you suspect? Who told you that?

ANGELO: They even made the question of my honesty the basis for the whole agreement.

MAURIZIO: Well, then, how could they want you—

ANGELO: Don't be stupid. Logic is one thing, the human animal another. You can quite easily propose a logical solution to something and at the same time hope in your heart of hearts that it won't work out. Believe me, I could easily ingratiate myself with them both by giving them a pretext for getting rid of me. I could, but I won't. I won't for their own sake. Because they can't possibly really want me to do that.

MAURIZIO: My God, you're incredible! You even deny them the possibility that they might want you to do something wrong?

ANGELO: Look. Let's suppose I went along. At first they'd be relieved. They'd be rid of the crushing weight of my presence. With me gone, they could tell themselves that the concept of honesty I failed to maintain survives, at least to some extent, in them. Agata would still be a married woman, now separated from an unworthy husband, and because her husband turned out to be a scoundrel, and because she's still a young woman, she would quite naturally allow herself to be consoled in the arms of an old friend. What would have been quite unthinkable for an unattached young lady is easily condoned in a married woman who has been absolved of her marriage vows. All right? So I, as the husband, could compromise my honesty and allow myself to be thrown out. But I didn't come into this house merely as a husband. As a husband and nothing else I would never have agreed to the proposition. There would have been no real need for me. I was needed here because the husband was soon to become a father. In a reasonable amount of time, that's understood. Here a father was desperately needed. And the father—oh, yes—the father has to remain an honest man. Not even

Fabio could want anything else. Because if, as the husband, I could leave here without hurting my wife, who would probably resume her maiden name, as a father I would do a terrible injury to the child, who can bear no other name but mine. In the eyes of the law and of society the boy is my son. And the lower I fall, the more he'll suffer from it. Fabio can't possibly want me to do such a thing.

MAURIZIO: No. You're quite right.

ANGELO: So you see? And you know what would happen to me. You know me, Maurizio: I'd sink like a stone. To avenge myself for the wrong they'd do me by publicly disgracing me, I'd want the child, who legally belongs to me. I'd leave the boy here for two or three years, then I'd prove that my wife is an adulteress living openly with her lover and I'd take the child away. Down, down into the mud with me . . . You know I have this horrible beast in me, this creature I freed myself from by chaining it here, in the conditions imposed by our agreement. It's in their own best interest to see that I continue to respect those conditions, as I firmly wish to do, because, once unchained, today or tomorrow, who knows where the beast will lead me, what will become of me? *(Suddenly changing tone.)* Well, that's enough of this. Tell me: did they send you to me the minute you got back? Come on, out with it! What were you supposed to ask me? Quickly, now! *(Looking at his watch.)* I've spent too much time with you already. You know the baby is being baptized this morning? And first I have a lunch here with my board of directors. Did Fabio send you? Or Mrs. Renni?

MAURIZIO: Well, yes . . . both of them. It's about the baptism, in fact. This name you insist on—

ANGELO *(with a sigh)*: Oh, I know.

MAURIZIO: Well, now—really!

ANGELO: I know, the poor little creature. He's too tiny for such a big name. He'll be crushed by it.

MAURIZIO: Sigismund!

ANGELO: But it's a very old family name. It was my father's . . . and my grandfather's . . .

MAURIZIO: Not an argument that makes much sense to them, you understand.

ANGELO: Or to me. You know, I might never have thought of it myself. But is it my fault? A horrible name, yes—ludicrous, especially for a child—and I confess—*(very softly)*—if he were my own son, really my son, I probably wouldn't have given it to him.

MAURIZIO: Ah, you see? You see?

ANGELO: See what? Under these circumstances what else can I call him? It's the same old story. It's not what I want; it's what appearances demand! The form, Maurizio, the form! You know that! Since I have to name him, I can't give him any name but this one! It's useless, you know! It's quite useless for them to insist! I'm sorry, but I will not give in. You can tell them that for me. And now I have to get back to work. This kind of thing is just a waste of time. I'm sorry to have to welcome you like this. Well, until later, eh? Good-by, Maurizio. *(He hurriedly shakes Maurizio's hand and exits into the studio.)*

(Maurizio stands there, not knowing what to do. After a moment or two Maddalena and Fabio enter softly, anxious to hear the news. Maurizio looks at them and helplessly scratches the back of his head. First Maddalena, then Fabio, nods to him questioningly, she with suffering eyes, he sullen and frowning. Maurizio shakes his head, then shrugs and spreads his

arms helplessly. Maddalena collapses into a chair and remains there, crushed. Fabio also sits down, but resentfully, his clenched fists resting on his knees. Maurizio now sits down, nodding thoughtfully, and sighs deeply several times. No one dares to break the crushing silence. Fabio snorts despairingly. Maddalena hardly breathes at all, but looks from one to the other, her expression more and more disconsolate. A long, long pause. Then Fabio bounds to his feet and begins to pace furiously up and down, clenching and unclenching his hands. After a moment or two Maurizio also rises, goes to Maddalena and bows, offering her his hand.)

MADDALENA *(softly, plaintively, taking his hand)*: You're going?

FABIO *(turning on them)*: Let him go! I don't know how he dares to show himself in this house! *(To Maurizio:)* Don't you ever set foot in here again!

MAURIZIO *(not daring to protest, turning just once to look at him, still holding Maddalena's hand, softly)*: Agata?

MADDALENA: In there, with the baby.

MAURIZIO: Please say good-by to her for me. *(He kisses Maddalena's hand, then turns away and spreads his arms wide.)* Tell her—tell her I'm sorry.

MADDALENA: Oh, she at least . . . she has the child now.

FABIO *(still pacing)*: Yes! And a fine time she'll have with it! Once the boy is old enough to fall under this maniac's spell!

MADDALENA: Yes! That's what I'm afraid of!

FABIO *(still pacing)*: It's already started with this business about the name!

MADDALENA *(to Maurizio)*: Believe me, Setti, it's been hell for ten months now!

FABIO *(still pacing)*: Imagine what kind of an education he'll want to give him!

MADDALENA: It's awful! We . . . we can't even read a newspaper any more.

MAURIZIO: No? Why not?

MADDALENA: Oh, he has some crazy idea about the press.

MAURIZIO: But . . . what's he like around the house? Harsh? Impolite?

MADDALENA: Nothing like that. Worse. He couldn't be more polite. He tells us to do the most dreadful things in the nicest possible way . . . giving such unexpected reasons and making them seem so unanswerable that we're always forced to give in to him. He's an appalling man, Setti, simply appalling! I can't even take a deep breath any more with him around!

MAURIZIO: My dear Mrs. Renni, what can I say? I'm absolutely annihilated! I never thought—

FABIO *(exploding again)*: You never thought! My God! I'd walk right out of here, if I didn't have to stay for the baptism! Don't you understand that I can't bear to listen to you? That I can't stand the sight of you?

MAURIZIO: You're right. Yes . . . I'll go, I'll go . . .

(The maid, a different girl from Act I, enters.)

MAID: The rector is here.

MADDALENA *(getting up)*: Ah, show him in.

(The maid exits.)

MAURIZIO: Good-by, Mrs. Renni.

MADDALENA: Must you really go? You won't stay for the baptism? Agata would be so happy. Well, come around, come around, Setti. I have great faith in you.

(Maurizio again spreads his arms helplessly, then bows, glances at Fabio without daring to say anything, and exits, nodding, as he goes, to the rector, who has just been admitted by the maid.)

MADDALENA: Come in, Father. Sit down.

RECTOR: My dear Mrs. Renni, how nice to see you!

FABIO: Good morning, Father.

RECTOR: Dear Mr. Colli! Mrs. Renni, I've come to make the final arrangements.

MADDALENA: Thank you, Father. Your assistant was here earlier.

RECTOR: Oh, excellent, excellent.

MADDALENA: Yes, and we've prepared everything in there. You were so kind to send us all those beautiful things from the church. It looks perfectly lovely! Adorable! Would you like to see—

RECTOR: And Mrs. Baldovino?

MADDALENA: Shall I call her?

RECTOR: Not if she's busy. I only wanted to know how she was.

MADDALENA: Fine now, thank you. All taken up with the baby, as you might imagine.

RECTOR: Of course.

MADDALENA: We can hardly tear her away.

RECTOR: And you, Mr. Colli, are the godfather?

FABIO: Uh . . . yes . . .

MADDALENA: And I'm the godmother!

RECTOR: Oh, I took that for granted! And—and the name? Is it to be that one—the one you—

MADDALENA: Unfortunately. *(She sighs.)*

FABIO *(angrily)*: Unfortunately!

RECTOR: Sigismund . . . Still, you know . . . after all . . . he was a saint . . . a king! I'm—I'm something of a dabbler in this field.

MADDALENA: Oh, we know! A scholar!

RECTOR: No, no! Nothing so exalted! Just a hobby of mine . . . Oh, yes . . . Saint Sigismund, King of Burgundy. Married Amalberga, daughter of Theodoric. She died and he was left a widower. He then married one of her ladies-in-waiting, I think. A terrible mistake. Horrible woman. She instigated him to commit—oh, yes—a dreadful crime—against his own son.

MADDALENA: My God! His own son? What did he do to him?

RECTOR: Well–*(a helpless gesture)*–he . . . he strangled him!

MADDALENA *(to Fabio)*: You hear that?

RECTOR *(quickly)*: But he repented, you know. At once. And to atone for his crime he dedicated himself to the strictest penitence. He retired to a monastery. Dressed only in sackcloth. And his many virtues stood him in good stead during his ordeal.

MADDALENA: His ordeal?

RECTOR: Yes, he was martyred. After being tortured, he was . . . *(He closes his eyes, bows his head, and then, with one finger, makes a gesture of decapitation.)* In the year 524, if I remember correctly.

FABIO: Oh, grand! A splendid saint! He strangles his own son and dies on the scaffold!

RECTOR: Very often the worst sinners, Mr. Colli, make the greatest saints. And this man was also a sage, you can take my word for it. He was the author of the celebrated *Lex Gombetta,* the Burgundian Code. At least that's one opinion. There are others, of course. But Savigny says he was, and when Savigny says something he's usually pretty reliable. Yes, yes, I'm with Savigny on that . . . a very reliable authority.

MADDALENA: At least, Father, I'll be able to call him by his diminutive, that's some consolation: Dino.

RECTOR: That's it, that's it: Dino! Excellent! A lovely name for a child! Goes well with the little fellow, eh, Mr. Colli?

MADDALENA: Yes. But who knows if he'll let us use it?

FABIO: Just what I was thinking.

RECTOR: Well, after all, if Mr. Baldovino insists on naming him after his father, who are we to object, eh? Well, now, what time shall we perform the ceremony?

MADDALENA: I suppose that's also up to him, Father. Wait. *(She rings for the maid.)* I'll tell him you're here. I think he's working. *(The maid enters.)* Tell Mr. Baldovino the rector is here. Ask him to come in for a moment. He's in the studio. *(She indicates the studio door. The maid goes to it, knocks, and enters. Immediately Angelo appears.)*

ANGELO *(entering hurriedly)*: Oh, Father, how nice of you to come! I'm honored! Please, please sit down.

RECTOR: The honor is mine. Thank you, Mr. Baldovino. I'm sorry to disturb you.

ANGELO: Not at all, not at all. I'm delighted to see you. What can I do for you?

RECTOR: We . . . I . . . if you'd be so kind . . . well, we–we wanted to agree on a time for the baptism, you know.

ANGELO: That's entirely up to you, Father. We're at your disposal. The godparents are both here, the nurse is in there, I'm ready any time, and the church is just down the street . . .

MADDALENA *(surprised)*: The church?

FABIO *(trying to control his anger)*: What's that?

ANGELO *(turning to look at them in astonishment)*: Did I say something wrong?

RECTOR *(quickly)*: You see, Mr. Baldovino, it was all arranged– You mean you don't know?

MADDALENA: We arranged everything in the nursery.

ANGELO: Arranged? Arranged what?

RECTOR: For the baptism. It was decided to have it here. It's often done nowadays.

FABIO: Everything necessary has been sent over from the church.

ANGELO: It's often done? I'm sorry, Father, but I never expected to hear you say such a thing.

RECTOR: Well, all I meant was . . . it's . . . it's become the fashion. All the best families, well . . . you know what I mean.

ANGELO *(smiling, quietly)*: And don't you think, Father, that it would be more fitting if we were to give an example of Christian humility, that spirit which recognizes that in God's eyes there are no distinctions between rich and poor?

MADDALENA: I don't see how we offend God by holding a baptism in our own home.

FABIO: Of course we don't! I'm sorry, but you always deliberately ruin everything! You never do anything anyone else wants to do! And I find it more than a little strange that you, of all people, should presume to preach to us!

ANGELO: Now, Mr. Colli, don't force me to raise my voice, please. What do you want from me? A profession of faith?

FABIO: No! I don't want anything from you!

ANGELO: If you think I'm being a hypocrite—

FABIO: I didn't say that! It just seems unnecessary, that's all!

ANGELO: And who are you to judge? What do you know about it? I suppose you think I shouldn't care at all how we baptize the child. But even if I didn't, it wouldn't matter in the least. The act doesn't concern me, but the child, and we all know it has to be done. And we all approve. Well, let's see that it's done correctly. The child must be baptized in church, at the baptismal font, and without claiming any special privileges that would serve only to contradict the whole spirit of the ceremony. I can't understand why you force me to say all this in front of the rector, who can't help but recognize that a baptism celebrated in the proper way, in its proper place, is a much more significant and devout event. Isn't that so, Father?

RECTOR: Oh, yes! Yes indeed! No doubt about it!

ANGELO: Furthermore, it's not only up to me. Since the matter concerns the child, let's hear what his mother has to say. *(He rings for the maid.)* You and I, Mr. Colli, will keep quiet. We'll leave it to the rector.

(The maid enters.)

Please ask Mrs. Baldovino to join us.

(The maid exits.)

RECTOR: Well . . . really, I . . . I'd rather let you do the talking, Mr. Baldovino. You do it so well.

ANGELO: No, no. I intend to stay out of it. You can explain how I feel and then—*(turning to Maddalena and Fabio)* —you can give your reasons. We'll let the mother make her own decision. And we'll do as she says. Here she is. *(Agata enters. She is pale, erect. Fabio and the rector rise. Angelo remains standing.)*

AGATA: Oh, the rector. Good morning, Father.

RECTOR: My warmest congratulations, Mrs. Baldovino.

FABIO *(bowing)*: Agata . . .

ANGELO *(to Agata)*: It's about the baptism. *(To the rector:)* You'll excuse me, Father. *(He exits into the studio.)*

AGATA: Hasn't it all been settled? I don't see—

MADDALENA: Yes, everything's ready. It looks so nice.

FABIO: It's him again!

RECTOR: Yes, you see, Mr. Baldovino—

MADDALENA: He says we can't baptize the baby here.

AGATA: Why not?

MADDALENA: Because he says . . . he says . . .

RECTOR: May I, Mrs. Renni? *(To Agata:)* Actually, he didn't say we can't do it. He left it up to you. Because, as he put it, it's really up to the mother to decide. So if you decide to have the baptism here—

MADDALENA: But of course! We were all agreed!
RECTOR: I really don't see any harm in it.
FABIO: All the best people are doing it now.
RECTOR: That's what I told Mr. Baldovino. Didn't I tell him that?
AGATA: Well? So what is there for me to decide?
RECTOR: Ah, you see . . . because Mr. Baldovino pointed out—and quite rightly, I must admit, with a sense of respect that does him the highest honor—he pointed out that the ceremony should more properly be celebrated in the church without claiming—oh, he put it so beautifully—without claiming any special privileges that would contradict the spirit of—of Christian humility—oh, a beautiful phrase, isn't it? A matter of principle, you see. Yes, a matter of principle.
AGATA: Well, Father, if you approve of what he says—
RECTOR: Oh, as a matter of principle I can't help but approve, Mrs. Baldovino.
AGATA: Then we'll have it in the church.
MADDALENA: Agata! You, too?
AGATA: I'm afraid he's right, Mother.
RECTOR: In principle, yes, of course. But if you—
FABIO: There's nothing wrong with doing it here.
RECTOR: Oh, of course not. Oh, there's nothing wrong with that.
FABIO: He just wants to ruin everything, as usual!
RECTOR: If you decide on the church, Mrs. Baldovino—
AGATA: Yes, I have decided, Father. In the church.
RECTOR: Very well, then. It's only down the street. All you have to do is let me know when. Any time, Mrs. Baldovino. Good day.
(To Maddalena:) Mrs. Renni.
MADDALENA: I'll see you out, Father.
RECTOR: Don't bother, please. Mr. Colli.
FABIO: Father.

RECTOR: There's no need—

MADDALENA: No, no, Father. No trouble. This way. *(They exit.)*

(Agata, very pale, is about to leave the room, but Fabio, unable to control himself, goes up to her and addresses her in a low, angry voice.)

FABIO: Agata, for God's sake, don't push me too far!

AGATA: Not now, Fabio. Please. *(She indicates the closed door into the studio.)*

FABIO: Always what he wants! Always!

AGATA: If what he wants is right—

FABIO: You've done everything, everything he wanted you to do! From the moment he set foot in this house!

AGATA: Let's not go back over all that, Fabio. We all agreed to this arrangement.

FABIO: But it's what you want now, isn't it? It's what you want! All you had to do was force yourself to swallow the original idea! And you did swallow it, that very first day, when you heard us talking! And now look at you! You accept everything, everything I had to force myself to do for your sake! You want it this way! You want him to know, you want him to know!

AGATA *(quickly)*: Know what?

FABIO: You see? You see? I'm right! You want him to know that we haven't touched each other since then! Don't you?

AGATA: For my own sake, Fabio.

FABIO: No! For his! For his sake!

AGATA: I couldn't bear to have him think otherwise.

FABIO: Oh, yes! Because you want him to respect you! As if he didn't agree to everything with us!

AGATA: And what does that mean? Nothing, except that we're all in this together. He's living up to his part of the bargain; I intend to live up to mine.

FABIO: But I want what belongs to me! What I have every

right to have, Agata! You! You! You! *(He seizes her and attempts to embrace her.)*

AGATA *(struggling to free herself)*: No! No! Stop it! Let go of me! I told you: I can't, I can't! Not until you get rid of him!

FABIO *(not letting her go)*: I will! I will! Today! I'll chase him out of here like the criminal he is!

AGATA *(stunned, unable to resist any longer)*: Criminal?

FABIO: Yes! Yes, a criminal! He's done it, Agata! He's been stealing from us!

AGATA: You're sure?

FABIO: Of course I'm sure! He's taken three million lire! I'll get rid of him today! And then we'll be together again! Darling– *(The studio door opens and Angelo appears. Finding them in each other's arms, he stops, surprised.)*

ANGELO: Oh, I beg your pardon. *(Severely, but with a shrewd smile.)* Good Lord, it's only me, you know, so it doesn't really matter. But it could have been the maid or somebody else. Next time lock the door.

AGATA *(angrily)*: There was absolutely no reason to!

ANGELO: Not for my sake, but for yours. *(To Fabio:)* Mr. Colli, you ought to know that.

AGATA: Exactly what I've been telling him. But now I think Fabio has something to say to you.

ANGELO: He does? Gladly. What is it?

AGATA *(scornfully)*: Don't you know?

ANGELO: Should I? *(Turning to Fabio.)* What is it?

AGATA: *(to Fabio)*: Tell him!

FABIO: No, not now.

AGATA: I want you to tell him now, in front of me!

FABIO: I think we ought to wait.

ANGELO *(scornfully)*: Perhaps you need witnesses?

FABIO: No, I don't need anyone! I know that you've stolen three million lire from us!

ANGELO *(very calmly, smiling)*: No, more. Much more. Something over five million. Wait. *(He takes out his wallet and extracts from it five notarized receipts which he glances over, adding them up.)* Yes, five million six hundred and seventy-two thousand, nine hundred and twenty-eight lire! Well over five million, Mr. Colli. You underestimated me.

FABIO: It doesn't matter, I don't care. You can keep the money and get out!

ANGELO: Not so fast, not so fast, Mr. Colli. I don't blame you for being in such a hurry, but the situation is much more serious than you think.

FABIO: Oh, come now! No more of your preaching!

ANGELO: I'm not preaching, no. *(Turning to Agata.)* I'd like you to hear this, if you don't mind. *(She looks at him, coldly silent. He turns back to Fabio.)* If you're anxious to make a thief out of me, perhaps we can reach some sort of agreement about that, too. But I want you to realize first that you aren't being fair to me. Look. *(He shows them the receipts, spreading them out like a fan.)* From these receipts, as you can see, Mr. Colli, the sum figures as savings and unexpected earnings of the syndicate I head. But that doesn't matter. We can fix all that. *(To Agata:)* All I had to do, you see, was stick these in my pocket and keep quiet. That's what they wanted me to do. *(Indicating Fabio and alluding to his partners.)* If I had fallen into the trap set for me by that crooked little man, that Marchetto Fongi who was here this morning. *(To Fabio:)* Oh, I don't deny the trap was set with a certain amount of skill. *(To Agata again:)* You don't understand these things, Agata, but they arranged it so that my personal accounts would show a large surplus, which I could have simply accepted without anyone finding out about it. Of course they expected me to fall for it and keep the money, at which point they would have produced other documents and caught me with my hand in the till. *(To Fabio:)* Isn't that how you planned it?

AGATA *(with barely disguised contempt, looking at the silent Fabio)*: Did you do this?

ANGELO *(quickly)*: No, Agata, you mustn't take it so hard!

AGATA: Not take it so hard?

ANGELO: If it upsets you so much, then—then I'm the one in trouble, not him.

AGATA: Why?

ANGELO: Because it means his situation has become intolerable. And if his is intolerable, mine is even worse.

AGATA: Worse? How can it be worse?

ANGELO *(gazing intently at her, then looking away, disturbed)*: Because . . . because if I were to become human . . . to become a man in your eyes, I . . . I couldn't go on. Oh, Agata the worst possible thing would happen to me: I . . . I'd no longer be able to look anyone in the face again . . . *(He passes a hand over his eyes and tries to control himself.)* No . . . enough of this. We have to find some solution and quickly. *(Bitterly.)* I thought I'd give myself the satisfaction today of making fools out of my directors, out of this Fongi. And out of you, too, Colli, for thinking you could trap me, a man like me, with such a childish scheme. But now I realize that if you had to stoop so low, to try to make a criminal out of me, just to get her back, without even understanding that my disgrace would reflect on your own son, well—the pleasure of honesty isn't worth it, not at that price. *(Holding the receipts out to Fabio.)* Here.

FABIO: What am I supposed to do with them?

ANGELO: Tear them up. They're the only proof I have. The money is in the safe, every cent of it. *(Looking him sternly in the eye, then speaking harshly, contemptuously.)* But you'll have to steal it yourself.

FABIO *(stung)*: Me?

ANGELO: Yes, you. You.

FABIO: Are you mad?

ANGELO: Why go halfway, Colli? I told you from the very beginning that if you wanted me to be an honest man, I'd be one. So now, if you want to make a criminal out of me, you'll have to commit the crime. You steal the money, I'll play the thief. And then I'll go away, because I know now I can't stay here any longer.

FABIO: You *are* mad!

ANGELO: You think so? From the beginning I've had to do the thinking here for all of us. I'm not suggesting you send me to jail. You couldn't do that. You'll take the money for me, that's all.

FABIO *(trembling, advancing on him)*: For you? What do you mean?

ANGELO: Don't be offended. Just my way of putting it. You'll cut a splendid figure, Colli. All you have to do is take the money out of the safe, just long enough to prove I stole it. Then you can put it back, so your investors won't suffer. After all, they put their trust in me out of their regard for you. It's clear, isn't it? I'll look like a criminal. That's all you want from me, isn't it?

AGATA *(violently)*: No! I won't let you do it! *(The two men stand facing each other. Then, to enhance the effect of her protest:)* And what about the baby?

ANGELO: We have to go through with this, Agata.

AGATA: No! I can't, I won't let you!

(The maid appears in the main entrance.)

MAID: The directors and Mr. Fongi.

FABIO *(quickly, dismayed)*: We'll talk about this tomorrow!

ANGELO *(readily, strongly, defiantly)*: I've made up my mind. You can go ahead right now!

AGATA: And I tell you I won't let you! Do you understand? I won't let you! I don't want you to!

ANGELO: All the more reason why I should.

FONGI *(entering with four directors)*: Excuse us. May we? *(Maddalena now enters, followed by the nurse carrying the baby. Everyone flocks around the infant with exclamations, congratulations, greetings, etc., while Maddalena proudly shows off the child.)*

CURTAIN

ACT III

The Renni-Baldovino living room the following morning. Angelo, dressed in the same shabby suit he first appeared in, is sitting with his elbows on his knees and his head in his hands, staring gloomily at the floor. Maddalena is talking to him urgently.

MADDALENA: But you don't have any right to do this, you ought to know that! It has nothing to do with either you or Fabio any more. Not even with her. It concerns the child, the child!

ANGELO *(looking up and staring at her ferociously)*: And what do I care about the child?

MADDALENA *(stunned, but quickly recovering)*: Oh, God, that's right. But I'm only reminding you of what you said yourself about the baby, that in the long run he would be the one to suffer the most. Blessed words. What an impression they made on my daughter and–

and what anguish they cause her, now that she's a mother and nothing but a mother! You ought to understand that.

ANGELO: I don't understand anything any more, Mrs. Renni.

MADDALENA: That's not true. You pointed it out to Fabio only yesterday.

ANGELO: What?

MADDALENA: That he couldn't go through with this because of the child.

ANGELO: I pointed it out? No, Mrs. Renni. I don't care what he did or what he'll do. I knew very well he'd try something like this. *(Looking at her, more irritated than contemptuous.)* And so did you, Mrs. Renni.

MADDALENA: I? No! No, I swear it!

ANGELO: What do you mean, no? Why else would he have organized this syndicate?

MADDALENA: I don't know. Perhaps—perhaps to give you something to do.

ANGELO: Yes, to get me out of the house. That was certainly the original purpose. He was hoping to keep me busy elsewhere, so that behind my back he and Agata could—

MADDALENA *(quickly interrupting)*: No, not Agata! Not her! Fabio, yes—that was probably what he wanted. But I can assure you that Agata—

ANGELO *(shrugging, impatiently)*: My God, are you so blind? You can really tell me this about her, to my face?

MADDALENA: It's the truth.

ANGELO: And doesn't it frighten you? *(A pause.)* Don't you understand what it means?

MADDALENA: What?

ANGELO: That I have to leave here and that, instead of coming to me, you should be trying to convince your daughter to let me go.

MADDALENA: But why? Why? I don't see—

ANGELO: Never mind why. The important thing is that I leave.

MADDALENA: No, no! She won't let you!

ANGELO: Please, Mrs. Renni, don't make me lose my head like the rest of you! Don't deprive me of my last remaining strength! I can still see the consequences of what others do blindly. Blindly, you know, not because they're all fools but because they live, and when you're alive, Mrs. Renni, you live and you don't see. I can see, because I came into this house in order *not* to live. Do you insist on bringing me back to life? Is that what you want? Be careful, because if life were to seize me in its grip and make me as blind as everybody else . . . *(He stops and makes a visible effort to overcome the onrush of his human feelings, the suppression of which always makes him look ferocious. Then he resumes, calmly, almost coldly:)* Look . . . look . . . all I wanted to do, quite simply, was point out to Colli the consequences of what he was about to do. That is, by wanting to make a thief out of an honest man—

MADDALENA: You?

ANGELO: Not me, not the real me, Mrs. Renni, but the man you all wanted in this house, the man I became, the man none of you understood. To make a thief out of such a man Colli himself would have to take the money.

MADDALENA: How can you expect him to do that?

ANGELO: He wants to make me look like a criminal.

MADDALENA: But he can't! He mustn't!

ANGELO: He'll take the money, I tell you! He'll pretend to steal it. If he doesn't, I will! Would you really force me to steal it?

(Maurizio, very worried, enters hurriedly. Angelo sees the expression on his face and laughs loudly.)

I suppose you're also here to beg me "not to commit this act of madness?"

MADDALENA *(quickly, to Maurizio)*: Yes, yes! Please, Setti, you persuade him!

MAURIZIO: Don't worry, Mrs. Renni. Of course he won't do it. Because he knows it's an act of madness. Not on his part, but on Fabio's.

ANGELO: Did he ask you to come here and fix everything?

MAURIZIO: Of course not! I'm here because you asked me to come. In your note last night. Don't you remember?

ANGELO: Oh, yes. And did you really bring me the money I asked you to loan me?

MAURIZIO: I didn't bring you a penny!

ANGELO: Because, like the bright fellow you are, you understood I was only bluffing? Good for you! *(He indicates the jacket he has on.)* However, you can see I'm dressed for departure—as I wrote you in my note—in the same suit I came in. But an honest man dressed like this, eh? What else can he want from an old school friend but a small loan in order to make a decent exit? *(He goes up to Maurizio and takes him by the arms.)* Remember, Maurizio, I've always been very particular about keeping up appearances.

MAURIZIO *(confused)*: What the devil are you talking about?

ANGELO *(turning to look at Maddalena and laughing again)*: Look at the way that poor woman stares at me . . . *(Friendly, casual.)* Now, I'll explain, Mrs. Renni. You see, the only real mistake Fabio made—and it's really quite understandable, I sympathize with him completely—was simply in thinking I would fall into his trap. The mistake is not irreparable. Colli will be made to understand that since I came into this house to play a game it amused me to play, I must play it out to the end. Yes, right up to the crime itself. But not a real crime, you understand. You can't actually expect me to pocket all that money, to really steal it. But the game is so enjoyable I'm willing to pretend to steal it. And don't worry, I mean about the threat I made: that in three or four years I'd come back and claim the child. I only said that to impress Colli. It's pure nonsense. What do I want with the child? Or were you afraid I'd blackmail you?

MAURIZIO: Go on, Angelo, stop it. No one thinks that.

ANGELO: And suppose it had occurred to me?

MAURIZIO: I said stop it!

ANGELO: No, not blackmail . . . But I did want to play the game out to this point, so I could enjoy the exquisite pleasure of seeing you all on your knees, begging me now not to take the money you all worked so hard to make me steal.

MAURIZIO: But you didn't steal it.

ANGELO: No. Because I want him to steal it, with his own hands.

(Fabio appears in the doorway, very upset and pale.)

And he will steal it, I promise you.

FABIO *(approaching Angelo in near terror)*: I *will* steal it? But then—oh, my God!—did you give—did you give anyone else the key to the safe?

ANGELO: No. Why?

FABIO: My God! My God! But then? Could anyone have found out? . . . Could Fongi have told anyone? . . .

MAURIZIO: Is the money missing?

MADDALENA: Good heavens!

ANGELO: Don't worry, Colli. It's not missing. *(He pats the inside pocket of his jacket.)* I have it.

FABIO: Ah, so you *did* take it?

ANGELO: I told you, I always go all the way in everything!

FABIO: What *are* you trying to do?

ANGELO: Don't worry. You see, I knew a gentleman like you would find it very difficult, perhaps impossible, to remove that money from the safe, even for a few minutes, even as a joke. So I went and took the money out of the safe last night.

FABIO: You did? And why, may I ask?

ANGELO: Why, to give you a chance, Colli, to make a magnificent gesture of restitution. Think of the effect on your board of directors!

FABIO: You still insist on this foolishness?

ANGELO: You see, I really did take the money. So now, if you won't do what I tell you, I'll stop pretending and we'll play the game for keeps. I'll be the criminal you wanted me to be.

FABIO: I only wanted to– But don't you understand? I've changed my mind. I don't want to go through with this.

ANGELO: But now I do want to go through with it.

FABIO: With what?

ANGELO: Exactly what you wanted. Didn't you tell Agata, right here, yesterday, that I had the money in my pocket? Well, I do have it in my pocket.

FABIO: But you haven't got me in your pocket, by God!

ANGELO: Yes, I do. You, too, Colli. And this morning I shall preside over our regular board meeting. I'm going to make my usual report. You can't stop me. Naturally, I'll say nothing about these surplus earnings Fongi so cleverly arranged and I'll give him the satisfaction of catching me red-handed. Oh, don't worry, I'll give a wonderful imitation of a criminal caught in the act. Then, later on, you and I will settle everything back here.

FABIO: You won't do it!

ANGELO: I will, I will, my dear Colli.

MAURIZIO: But you can't just voluntarily pretend you're a thief when you aren't one!

ANGELO *(firmly, threateningly)*: I told you I've made up my mind. I'll actually steal the money if you persist in opposing me!

FABIO: But why? In God's name, why? If I myself beg you not to do this?

ANGELO *(turning to look at him and speaking in a low, serious tone)*: And how can you expect me to remain in this house any longer, Colli?

FABIO: I told you I was sorry—really sorry . . .

ANGELO: For what?

FABIO: For what I've done.

ANGELO: But there's no need to be sorry for what you've done, my dear Colli, because it's only natural—but for what you haven't done!

FABIO: And what should I have done?

ANGELO: What should you have done? Why, after a few months you should have immediately come to me and told me that even if I wanted to abide by our agreement, which was costing me nothing, and you wanted to abide by it, which was only natural, there was someone else in this house who counted more than either of us, someone whose dignity and nobility of spirit made it impossible for us to go on with this farce. And then I would at once have shown you how absurd the whole idea was, that any honest man could lend himself to such an arrangement.

FABIO: Yes, yes, you're right! *(Indicating Maurizio:)* In fact, I was angry with him for having brought someone like you here!

ANGELO: No, he was absolutely right to bring me, believe me! What did you want in this house? An honest mediocrity? As if any ordinary man would accept such an arrangement, unless he were a scoundrel. I was the only one able to accept it. Just as I'm able, you see, to accept the idea of passing for a thief.

MAURIZIO: But how can you? Why?

FABIO: Why? Just for the fun of it?

MAURIZIO: Who's forcing you to? No one wants you to do it!

MADDALENA: No one! We're all begging you not to!

ANGELO *(to Maurizio)*: You, out of friendship . . . *(To Maddalena:)* You, because of the child . . . *(To Fabio:)* And you? What's your reason?

FABIO: The same as hers.

ANGELO *(looking into his eyes)*: The child? That's all? Nothing else?

(Fabio does not answer.)

I'll tell you the real reason: because you realize now the effect of what you've done. *(To Maddalena:)* Mrs. Renni, you think he's concerned with the good name of the child? An illusion! *(Indicating Maurizio:)* He knows that my past . . . unfortunately . . . yes, that my present way of life . . . the birth of a child . . . might help to bury the memory of so many other sad events . . . my old life. . . . *(Indicating Fabio:)* But now he has a lot more to think about than just the child, Mrs. Renni. Oh, a lot more. *(Turning to the others:)* And what about me? Don't I count for anything? Do you think I can stay here forever, a light by which you can all see and nothing else? I, too, am made of flesh and bone. I, too, have blood in my veins—a thick, black blood, bitter with the poison of my memories. And I'm afraid! Yes, I'm afraid! Yesterday, in here, when this man, in front of your daughter, hurled his accusations in my face, I fell blindly—more blindly than any of you—into another and far more subtle trap, a trap that has been lying in wait for me during the ten months I've been in this house, living with a woman I hardly dared even to look at. And this childish little trick of yours, Colli, was all I needed to make me aware of the abyss at my feet. . . .

I planned to keep quiet, you understand? To swallow your insult in front of her, to let her think I was a criminal. Then I would get you alone and prove to you it wasn't true, and force you in secret to play our game out to the end. But I was unable to keep quiet. My flesh cried out in protest! And you . . . she . . . all three of you . . . can you still dare to prevent me from doing what I must do? . . . I tell you that to resist this force within me I am compelled to steal that money!

(They all look at him in silence. A pause. Agata, pale and determined, now enters. She takes a few steps into the room and stops. Angelo looks at her. He tries to remain composed and grave, but his eyes betray a hint of terror.)

AGATA *(to her mother, Fabio, and Maurizio)*: I want to talk to him. Alone.

ANGELO *(almost stuttering, his eyes lowered)*: No. No, please. You see, I—

AGATA: I must talk to you.

ANGELO: It's . . . it's useless, Agata . . . I told them . . . I told them all I had to say.

AGATA: And now you'll hear what I have to say.

ANGELO: No, no . . . please . . . It's useless, I tell you. Enough . . . enough . . .

AGATA: I insist. *(To the others:)* Please leave us alone.
(They exit.)
I didn't come here to tell you not to go . . . I came to tell you that if you do go, I'll go with you.

ANGELO *(he appears about to faint, then barely recovers. He speaks very softly)*: I understand. You don't want to beg me for the child's sake. A woman like you doesn't ask for sacrifices; she makes them.

AGATA: I'm not making any sacrifice. I'm only doing what I must.

ANGELO: No, no, Agata, you can't. Not for the baby's sake

nor for yours. And at any cost I must prevent you.

AGATA: You can't, I'm your wife. You wish to leave? Fine. I approve and I'll follow you.

ANGELO: Where? What are you saying? Have pity on yourself, and on me . . . and don't make me tell you . . . try to understand by yourself, because I . . . because I . . . face to face with you I . . . I don't know what to say . . .

AGATA: There's nothing else to say. Everything you said that first day you came here was enough for me. I should have come in at once and offered you my hand.

ANGELO: Oh, if you only had, Agata! I swear to you I hoped for a moment that you would. I mean, come in . . . I would never have dared even to touch your hand . . . but it would have ended right there.

AGATA: You wouldn't have accepted?

ANGELO: No. Out of shame, Agata, out of shame. Face to face with you, as I'm ashamed now.

AGATA: Of what? Of having spoken honestly?

ANGELO: That's easy, Agata. It's very easy to be honest, you see, as long as it's only a question of saving appearances. If you had come into the room that day to tell me you couldn't go through with the deception, I couldn't have stayed here a minute longer. As I can't stay here now.

AGATA: So you thought I agreed with Fabio?

ANGELO: No, Agata. But I waited, and when you didn't come in . . . But I spoke that way only to show him that to expect me to be honest was impossible. . . . Not for me . . . but for all of you! . . . So you ought to realize that now–since you've changed the conditions–it becomes impossible for me . . . Not because I don't want to be honest, but because of what I am . . . because of all I've done. . . . You see, only the part I agreed to play here in your house–

AGATA: We asked you to play it!

ANGELO: And I accepted.

AGATA: But you warned us in advance what the consequences would be. You tried to dissuade him. Well, I accepted, too.

ANGELO: And you shouldn't have, you shouldn't have, Agata. That was your mistake. My voice was never heard in this house. Never. It was only the voice of a grotesque mask I chose to wear. And why? Here you were, all three of you, a portion of this poor suffering humanity of ours, exulting in the joys and undergoing the torments of living. In this house a poor, weak mother had made the sacrifice of allowing her daughter to have an illicit love affair! And you, in love with a good man, allowed yourself to ignore the fact that this man was already married to someone else. You all realized you had done wrong, that you were to blame. And so you tried to escape the consequences of your action by bringing me into your house. And I came, speaking a language in these rooms that stifled and paralyzed you—the language of an abstract concept, a fictitious and unnatural honesty which you finally had the courage to rebel against. I knew very well that in the long run neither Fabio nor your mother would accept the conditions of such an arrangement. Their humanity was bound to rebel against it. I heard their groans and protests. And believe me, I enjoyed watching them intrigue against the most serious of the consequences I had told them to expect right from the very beginning. But it was dangerous for you, Agata. The only danger I could see was that you'd accept all the consequences, to the bitter end. And you did accept them. In fact, you were able to accept them because, unfortunately for you, the moment you became a mother the young girl in love died, she simply ceased to exist. Now, more than anything else, you are a mother. But I—I'm not the father of your child, Agata. Do you understand what that means?

AGATA: Then it's for the child's sake you want to go away? Because you aren't the real father?

ANGELO: No, no! What are you saying? Try to understand! By the very fact that you'd want to come with me you make the child mine, more sacred to me than if he were my own son—the pledge of your sacrifice and your esteem.

AGATA: Well, then?

ANGELO: But I tell you this only to remind you of my own reality, Agata. Because you can see nothing but your child! You're still talking to a mask, the mask of a father.

AGATA: No, no. I'm talking to you, to the man behind that mask!

ANGELO: And what do you know about me? Who I am?

AGATA: This is what you are. The man I see before me.

(Overwhelmed, Angelo bows his head.)

You can raise your head and look at me, Angelo, as I can look at you. Otherwise, in your presence we'd all have to lower our eyes. If only because, of all of us, you had the courage to be ashamed of what you had done with your life.

ANGELO: I never thought I'd hear anyone speak to me like this. *(Violently, as if recovering from a spell.)* No . . . no . . . Agata . . . please go! Believe me, I'm not worth it! Do you know what I have here? In my pocket? I—I have more than five million lire!

AGATA: You'll return the money and we'll go away.

ANGELO: Return it? Do you think I'm crazy? I won't return it! Not—one—cent—of—it!

AGATA: All right, then the child and I will follow you down that road as well.

ANGELO: You—you'd come with me—even . . . even as a

criminal? *(He collapses into a chair. He hides his face in his hands and weeps.)*

AGATA *(she looks at him for a moment, then goes to the door and calls)*: Mother!

(Maddalena enters, sees Angelo weeping, and stops, dumfounded.)

You can tell those gentlemen we have no further use for them here.

ANGELO *(immediately rising)*: No, wait! . . . The money! *(He tries to control himself, to dry his tears, but he can't find his handkerchief. At once Agata offers him hers. He understands the significance of this act which, by its very simplicity, unites them for the first time. He kisses the handkerchief and dabs at his eyes as he stretches out his hand to her. Then he gains control of himself with a deep sigh that expresses immense joy.)* Yes, I know now. I know what to tell them!

CURTAIN